Humor Writing

Humor Writing

Activities for the English Classroom

Bruce A. Goebel
Western Washington University

NCTE
National Council of Teachers of English
1111 W. Kenyon Road, Urbana, Illinois 61801-1096

Staff Editor: Bonny Graham
Manuscript Editor: JAS Group
Interior Design: Jenny Jensen Greenleaf
Cover Design: Pat Mayer
Cover Image: iStockphoto.com / Ricardo Infante Alvarez

NCTE Stock Number: 22136

It is the policy of NCTE in its journals and other publications to provide a forum for the open discussion of ideas concerning the content and the teaching of English and the language arts. Publicity accorded to any particular point of view does not imply endorsement by the Executive Committee, the Board of Directors, or the membership at large, except in announcements of policy, where such endorsement is clearly specified.

Every effort has been made to provide current URLs and email addresses, but because of the rapidly changing nature of the Web, some sites and addresses may no longer be accessible.

Library of Congress Cataloging-in-Publication Data

Goebel, Bruce A., 1958–
Humor writing : activities for the English classroom / Bruce A. Goebel.
p. cm.
Includes bibliographical references and index.
ISBN 978-0-8141-2213-6 (pbk.)
1. Wit and humor—Authorship. 2. Comedy—Authorship. I. Title.
PN6149.A88G64 2011
808.7071'2—dc23

2011019311

For Brenda, who has put up with my sense of humor for more than thirty years.

Contents

Permission Acknowledgments

Excerpt from "Skunk Dog," pp. 18–19 from THEY SHOOT CANOES, DON'T THEY by Patrick F. McManus. Copyright © 1982 by Patrick F. McManus. Reprinted by arrangement with Henry Holt and Company, LLC.

Excerpt from "My First Deer, and Welcome to It" from THEY SHOOT CANOES, DON'T THEY by Patrick F. McManus. Copyright © 1982 by Patrick F. McManus. Reprinted by arrangement with Henry Holt and Company, LLC.

"homage to my hips": Copyright © 1987 by Lucille Clifton. Reprinted by permission of Curtis Brown, Ltd.

"Litany," copyright © 2002 by Billy Collins, from NINE HORSES by Billy Collins. Used by permission of Random House, Inc.

"Everybody Tells Me Everything": Copyright © 1940 by Ogden Nash. Reprinted by permission of Curtis Brown, Ltd.

"News Item," copyright 1926, renewed © 1954 by Dorothy Parker, from THE PORTABLE DOROTHY PARKER by Dorothy Parker, edited by Marion Meade. Used by permission of Viking Penguin, a division of Penguin Group (USA) Inc.

"You Take the High Dive" by Richard Armour from *Writing Light Verse and Prose Humor*. Reprinted with permission of the Estate of Richard Armour.

"Aspiring DJ" from HIPSTER HAIKU by Siobhan Adcock, copyright © 2006 by Siobhan Adcock. Used by permission of Broadway Books, a division of Random House, Inc.

Excerpt from "Duct Tape Psalm" by Greg Keeler from *American Falls* (Confluence Press, 1987). Reprinted by permission.

Excerpt from "Swiss Army Sermon" by Greg Keeler from *Epiphany at Goofy's Gas* (Dark City Press, 1991). Reprinted by permission.

"Shoem" by Liz Brownlee, first published in *The Apple-Raid* chosen by Pie Corbett (Macmillan, 2001). Reprinted by permission.

"Dover Beach" by Bill Greenwell. Reprinted by permission. For this and other short poems, see Greenwell's website at http://www.billgreenwell.com/poems/display_poem.php?key_id=509.

"The Princess and the Pea" from DR. JOHNSON'S WATERFALL by Helen Bevington. Copyright 1946 by Helen Bevington. Copyright © renewed 1974 by Helen Bevington. Reprinted by permission of Houghton Mifflin Harcourt Publishing Company. All rights reserved.

"This Is Just to Say" by William Carlos Williams, from THE COLLECTED POEMS: VOLUME 1, 1909–1939, copyright © 1938 by New Directions Publishing Corp. Reprinted by permission of New Directions Publishing Corp.

"This Is Just to Say" © 2002 by Garrison Keillor. Used with permission. All rights reserved.

From POETRY FOR CATS by Henry Beard, copyright © 1994 by Henry Beard and John Boswell Associates. Used by permission of Villard Books, a division of Random House, Inc.

Acknowledgments

I would like to thank Western Washington University for the professional leave that allowed me to complete this project. I also owe a debt of gratitude to my sons, Elliott and Russell, who scour the Internet for the most recent viral humor and comic memes, and then share them with me. This has allowed me to appear far more hip than I really am. Most of all, I would like to thank my students, who have so kindly laughed at my lame jokes, offered insightful and often hilarious suggestions, and served as captive lab rats for the activities in this book.

Introduction

A person without a sense of humor is like a wagon without springs. It's jolted by every pebble on the road.

—Henry Ward Beecher

You can turn painful situations around through laughter. If you can find humor in anything, even poverty, you can survive it.

—Bill Cosby

In this time of high-stakes tests and school accountability, English classrooms have been pushed to become increasingly serious places. When combining No Child Left Behind (NCLB) pressures to improve basic reading and writing skills with our own desires to use literature and writing to do important cultural work—such as fighting ethnic, gender, and social class discrimination—humor is virtually banned from the classroom. In fact, when I talk with experienced and preservice teachers, there seems to be a palpable fear of using class time for "fun." Mary Kay Morrison refers to this as *humorphobia* and lists its symptoms:

- Fear of not having time for humor because of accountability expectations.
- Fear of being perceived as silly, unproductive, an airhead, and unprofessional.
- Fear of losing "control" of the class or loss of discipline.
- Fear of inadequacy or inability to tell a joke coupled with inexperience in the use of humor.

- Fear of punishment or retaliation in an environment that is hostile or unaccustomed to humor.
- Fear of being made fun of or being the brunt of jokes. (72)

This phobia is unfortunate because humor can benefit teachers and students in many ways, from the personal to the educational.

For decades, medical studies have shown that humor and laughing lead to a host of positive health benefits, including improving respiration, circulation, the body's immune system, and pain tolerance, as well as reducing stress. Beyond the physiological benefits, humor can also contribute to mental health. Studies indicate that positive (as opposed to demeaning) humor can lead to a greater sense of well-being, perceptions of mastery and control, and a reduction in anxiety, depression, and anger (R. Martin 305). If we think about classroom management for a moment and consider the causes of many student disruptions—ones rooted in anger, anxiety, and low self-esteem—positive humor is in many ways a direct response to these problems. If we think about the general goal of helping students lead healthy lives, then we might consider psychologist Rod Martin's claim that a "sense of humor is an important component of overall mental health. People who are psychologically well-adjusted, with satisfying personal relationships, tend to use humor in ways that enhance their own well-being and closeness to others" (306).

Though on the surface these benefits seem beyond the purview of the English classroom, they are important nevertheless. We are used to the idea of cautioning students about the health problems related to such things as substance abuse, eating disorders, risky sexual behaviors, and the like, because they have such obvious consequences. But in many ways, this approach is a bit like an insurance company that will pay for major medical crises but refuses to fund the kinds of wellness programs that might circumvent many of these problems in the first place. As the epigraphs of this introduction suggest, humor can be a healthy outlet that helps one cope with life struggles. In Sherman Alexie's young adult novel, *The Absolutely True Diary of a Part-Time Indian*, the narrator says that he takes his drawing of humorous cartoons seriously because "I use them to understand the world. I use them to make fun of the world" (95). In a life filled with poverty, substance abuse, and the death of loved ones, he turns, at least in part, to humor for salvation.

But what does any of this have to do with teaching? Significantly, humor has many benefits specific to the classroom. When students are asked to list the most important characteristics of an effective teacher, having a sense of humor consistently ranks toward the top. This likely stems from a couple of side effects of humor. First, as Rod Martin explains,

> The value of humor in the classroom may be particularly related to its role in promoting a sense of immediacy. Immediacy is an educational concept referring to the degree to which a teacher makes a close personal connection with students, as opposed to remaining distant and aloof. (353)

In other words, shared positive humor tends to create personal bonds between students and teacher, and between students of differing backgrounds. Or, as Claudia Cornett notes, "Laughter decreases social distance among people and causes a feeling of connectedness. Rapport is built by laughing together" (37).

This sense of immediacy leads directly to the second classroom benefit: a reduction in student anxiety. As researchers Neelam Kher, Susan Molstad, and Roberta Donahue point out, "By reducing anxiety, humor improves student receptiveness to alarming or difficult material, and ultimately has a positive affect [sic] on test performance" (401). When students feel personally connected to the teacher and to other students, they are more willing to take risks and engage with challenging material without being overly concerned with failure. In fact, some research shows that student performance increases by nearly 10 percent when teachers judiciously use humor (a few times per class) in a way specifically related to key points in the lesson (Ziv).

However, while these effects may be true for any content area, humor can play an even more central role in an English classroom. Young adults admire people with a humorous wit, just as they are attracted to comic media such as *Saturday Night Live* and *The Daily Show*, and to the performances of innumerable stand-up comedians. The popularity of many novels rests often in their use of humor—from slapstick in J. K. Rowling's Harry Potter series to the angry, ironic humor in Laurie Halse Anderson's *Speak* to the self-deprecating humor of *The Absolutely True Diary of a Part-Time Indian*. This is to say that while many aspects of the English curriculum may lack an appeal for certain students, humor almost always gets an enthusiastic reception. That's important because, according to Cornett, student interest in particular reading material accounts "for 30 times the variance in reading success, and humor provokes interest. Potentially serious literacy problems can be addressed using a curriculum riddled with fun" (16).

And let's remember that humor is nothing less than the careful and effective use of language. This is one of the reasons we value the work of humor writers from Mark Twain to J. D. Salinger to Alexie. Most humor relies heavily on figurative language and wordplay and involves linguistic problem solving, the natural arenas of the English classroom. In addition, in a school climate increasingly concerned with convergent thinking and finding the right answer, humor challenges students to think divergently, creatively, and to welcome an array of possibilities (Nason).

Humor may also be an important component of differentiation in the English classroom. In his article "Humor: A Course Study for Gifted Learners," Richard Shade argues that because much humor requires careful attention to and a deftness with language, gifted students are often particularly adept in the reading and production of humorous texts. He suggests that the close relationship between humor and creativity "allows an individual to 'jump the track' or 'think outside the box' more successfully" and to be more receptive to the kinds of risk taking that bright students need if they are to feel intellectually challenged (47). Similarly, because positive humor tends to relieve anxiety and build trust in the classroom, English language learning (ELL) educators such as Stephen Cary argue that it is helpful in establishing a classroom environment that invites language sharing and experimentation (77). Cary suggests that teachers working with ELL students should be

> encouraging more student jokes and funny stories;
>
> telling more jokes and funny stories themselves;
>
> increasing the number of humorous read-aloud books;
>
> sharing a daily cartoon or comic strip;
>
> sharing a daily humorous video clip. (78)

Given that one of the primary goals of the ELL classroom is to increase fluency, such sharing directly contributes to student progress.

All of which is to say that humor has a justified place in the English classroom. But don't worry—this is not a book that will implore you to learn how to be funny, delivering appropriate one-liners at the right times (see Ronald Berk's books for ideas on that approach). In fact, the only things *my* students usually find funny about me are my feeble attempts to be funny ("All right, class, for this next activity I'd like you to work in pairs, or apples if you'd prefer"). Rather, I'm suggesting making humor a part of the curriculum itself. In general, I try to intersperse activities in humor throughout my units, using them in part as a kind of comic relief for the serious work we do, but also for the specific skills that an exploration into humor can impart: skills in grammar and conventions, in voice and style, in figurative language, and in what I like to call *reading like a writer*. These activities provide students with a fun way to improve as readers and writers, and offer them the rare opportunity to express their humorous sides in an increasingly serious classroom space.

This book explores more than 150 activities that teachers might use to incorporate humor into the curriculum. It is divided into four chapters: (1) "Humorous Words, Phrases and Sentences," (2) "Funny Stories and Essays," (3) "Light Verse," and (4) "Parody." Within each chapter, I offer definitions, examples, and suggested activities.

Chapter 1 begins with a focus on what I call *language humor*, the building blocks of comic writing, and looks first at funny-sounding words, slang, portmanteaus, puns, oronyms, and daffynitions. The activities in this section provide students with an opportunity to explore the role that sound plays in our appreciation of language, as well as a chance to explore the figurative language we use to coin new words and describe our world in a new way. In looking at puns, students also are introduced to the fundamental elements of humor, such as incongruity and surprise. The second section of Chapter 1 examines humor connected to playful use of various parts of speech, odd syntax in word combinations, and errors in grammar and conventions. It starts with the ways verbs, adjectives, and adverbs can function metaphorically, and then shifts to a look at the ways such things as ambiguous pronouns, misplaced modifiers, and typos can intentionally and unintentionally create humorous sentences. The final section of this chapter examines jokes, with particular attention to a few of the common strategies that joke writers use, such as the rule of three, reversal, misdirection, exaggeration, lists, and definitions.

Humorous stories and essays are the focus of Chapter 2. I begin with a few building blocks—creating comic characters, conflicts, and plots—and then follow those with an exploration of how to apply such common narrative humor strategies as exaggeration, slapstick, and irony. The chapter ends with a look at the basic structure and strategies for comic essays and other potentially humorous nonfiction forms. More than the other chapters, this one takes a sequential approach much like a unit plan, beginning with prewriting strategies, and working through to drafting process, all focusing on helping students develop amusing material and story outlines.

Chapter 3 explores humorous poetry, starting with ways of introducing poetic elements such as metaphor, alliteration, and meter from a comic perspective. Along the way, I offer examples from some of the famous writers of light verse, from Ogden Nash and Dorothy Parker to Billy Collins. The chapter ends with an exploration of a variety of poetic forms that can be put to humorous use, including quatrains, haiku, clerihews, and more.

Because it examines parody, Chapter 4 incorporates aspects of the first three chapters. Beginning with an extended definition of the various forms and intentions that parody can take, the chapter moves through activities that focus on poetry, fiction, and nonfiction. In the process, students will explore how to recognize a text, author, or genre's distinctive form and style; summarize a text and identify important or repeating ideas, images, and symbols; imitate in writing the form, style, or content of a text, genre, or author; and apply strategies of incongruity, reversal, misdirection, punning and wordplay, and exaggeration. The chapter ends with a focus on the parodying of forms common to everyday lives of secondary students—teen magazines, textbooks, exams, lunch menus, and the like.

There are two primary ways a teacher might want to use the activities in this book: (1) as discrete, five-to-ten-minute activities spread throughout the curriculum for comic relief, or (2) as a sequenced curriculum for a unit on humor writing. A teacher interested in the first approach might select from any of the activities in Chapter 1, as well as the final five poetry activities in Chapter 3 and the nonfiction activities in Chapter 4. For a teacher who would like to create a three-to-four-week humor writing unit, I recommend the following sequence:

Chapter 1
- The Rule of Three
- Reversals
- Misdirection
- Exaggeration

Chapter 2
- Extended Exaggeration
- Slapstick
- Irony and Sarcasm
- The Humorous Essay

Chapter 3
- Alliteration
- Onomatopoeia
- Metaphor and Simile
- Rhyme
- Feet and Meter
- Couplets
- Quatrains

Chapter 4
- Parody of Poetry
- Parodic Quotations
- Parodic Condensation
- Parodic Adaptation

If one has the luxury of more than a few weeks to dedicate to a unit on humor writing, then returning to writing funny stories in Chapter 2, and fiction and nonfiction parody in Chapter 4 could extend the unit. Regardless of whether the activities are taken piecemeal or as a sequence, the activities in this book are intended to provide a bit of comic relief in the classroom, to introduce students to the diverse and exciting field of humor studies, and to give them the rare opportunity to write in their own voices in a divergently creative way.

Regardless of which approach a teacher might take, a word of caution is in order. Because much humor intentionally transgresses boundaries and often uses people as the target of jokes, it presents a potential danger for the secondary English classroom. Students should not be making fun of each other, their teachers, staff, or administrators, no matter how well intentioned. This isn't to say that they cannot make fun of high school culture in general, or the stereotypes of adolescents and teachers with which they are all familiar. But I suggest the following rule:

> No humor shared in class may target *specific* individuals in this school district, with the exception of your being allowed to make fun of yourself.

Throughout this book I make suggestions on how teachers might direct student humor toward more general or public targets. This is a fine line, however. For example, in Chapter 2 I discuss the drafting of a humorous essay about the general behavior of some boys at school dances. Although there is no specific target for this essay, it is possible that a few boys might be annoyed by it—but probably not as annoyed as when they are told to read *Paradise Lost*. The same thing is true in the selecting of humorous texts for reading purposes. The appropriateness of humor is a judgment call, one that you and your students will need to make.

1

Humorous Words, Phrases, and Sentences

A joke is not a thing, but a process, a trick you play on the listener's mind. You start him off toward a plausible goal, and then by a sudden twist you land him nowhere at all or just where he didn't expect to go.

—*Max Eastman*

Whatever is funny is subversive.

—*George Orwell*

Humor Defined

As the old saw goes, as soon as you try to explain humor, it's no longer funny. Or, as E. B. White said, "Analyzing humor is like dissecting a frog. Few people are interested and the frog dies of it." However, I have not come to bury humor, but to praise it, so we'll keep the definition short and the examples long. Although definitions of humor differ somewhat, depending on whether one approaches it from a psychological, anthropological, or literary perspective, most scholars agree that it is rooted in *expectation and surprise*.

By nature, human beings are pattern-seeking creatures. Consciously and subconsciously, we order our lives in ways that set up expectations. Each day I'll get up and make coffee, ride my scooter to work, teach, and then write. When I get home, my living room will be there with the couch under the big window, my teenage son slouching on it, book in hand, potato-chip crumbs sprinkled like snowflakes around him. I'll ask him, "How's it going?" He'll grunt. These things are a pattern—boring perhaps—but a pattern. And this pattern sets up expectations. We could express this mathematically in one of those "Which number comes next: 3, 6, 9, __" problems, or logically in one of those "Which item doesn't fit: mop, broom, vacuum, orange" questions. We see patterns everywhere, and these patterns set up continual expectations.

One of the fundamental aspects of humor is that it disrupts these expectations. It violates our logical perceptions of the normal. It generally does this through *incongruity,* which might be defined as the placing together of two or more things in a way that does not fit expectations. Such a break in the pattern generates surprise. If my coffee has a fish in it, if my scooter suddenly flies, if my son is vacuuming the living room, my daily pattern is broken, and I respond emotionally from the shock. If the surprise is humorous, I laugh. If it is annoying, I rant. If it is tragic, I cry.

Of course, if the surprise is annoying or tragic and it happens to someone else, then it may well be humorous to me. Or, as comedian Mel Brooks said "Tragedy is when I cut my finger. Comedy is when you walk into an open sewer and die." This leads to another aspect of humor: it can be hostile. Whether playfully self-deprecating or virulently abusive, most humor has a *target*. Someone or something is the butt of the joke. If the target of the humor is someone, something, or some value representative of a disempowered group, and the joke is told by a representative of a group in power, then the humor is oppressive. America's long tradition of racist and sexist jokes was (and continues to be) largely a means of psychologically justifying unjust treatment. If, on the other hand, the target is someone, something, or some value representative of a group in power, and the joke is told by someone disempowered, then the humor is subversive. Recent humor by female, gay, lesbian, and "ethnic" comedians often takes subversion as a primary tactic.

There is, as teachers well know, a danger here. It may be fine when the humor makes fun of cats, or Tom Cruise, or school lunches. But in a classroom, it may be altogether unacceptable (depending on the degree of hostility) when the humor attacks the school's principal, an ethnic group, or a specific student in the class. Humor is powerful. For that reason alone, perhaps, it deserves study in the English classroom, but with some caution.

Regardless of whether humor is subversive or oppressive, positive or neutral or negative in relation to its target, it is most simply defined as a surprising incongruity that evokes laughter (or at least bemusement). As simple as this definition is, however, there are myriad ways to create literary humor, ranging from funny-sounding words to the complex plots of a Shakespearean comedy. Let's start small, with words, phrases, and sentences. But as we look at ways to help students understand and generate humor, keep in mind that creating humor is challenging. Comedian Drew Carey said that a good stand-up comic might keep one out of ten jokes that he or she writes. For those of us less professional, our "success" rate is likely to be even lower. It's important for students to understand two things:

1 Not every attempt they make will be funny, perhaps not even most, and that's okay.
2 They increase the likelihood of humorous success with each extra attempt they make at creating a pun or a joke or a story lead.

In other words, it's the process that counts. The prewriting, drafting, and revising, the starts and stops, and the experiments for the fun of it are all crucial to humor writing.

Language Humor

Language humor relies on the sounds of words, words with multiple meanings, unusual word combinations, and unusual syntax. The most rudimentary examples of such humor can be found in abundance in the nonsense words of children's literature and songs. Shirley Ellis's "The Name Game" or, as it is also known, "The Banana Song," might have as its first verse, "Shirley Shirley bo burley / Banana fana fo firley / Fe fi fo firley / SHIRLEY!" We derive pleasure from such a song (or at least we used to) simply because of the musical sound play and the resistance the sounds have to normal meaning.

We find a slightly more complicated version of this in the Lewis Carroll poem "Jabberwocky." The opening lines, "'Twas brillig, and the slithy toves / did gyre and gimble in the wabe," amuse and puzzle us with the ways such words as *brillig*, *toves*, and *wabe* resemble real words, but resist clear interpretation. Though today, such language play might not induce adolescents and adults to laugh out loud as we once might have, it nevertheless suggests that language and syntax can be inherently amusing. To that end, let's look at a progression of language humor, moving roughly from simple to more complex.

Slang

We might begin with the single words or short word combinations that generate humor through sound, incongruity, or instability. It only takes a moment in the school hallway to recognize the love young adults have for *slang*. Though worthy of historical study in and of itself, I turn to slang for its comic potential. Slang tends to play off either humorous sounds or an implied metaphorical incongruity, or both. Take a look at a few slang terms from the past eighty years as listed in Tom Dalzell's *Flappers 2 Rappers* (Figure 1.1).

Slang of the 1930s	Slang of the 1950s	Slang of the 1980s
booshwash—empty talk, false gasper—a cigarette lulu—something very good pill—disagreeable person	cat—a hip person horn—the telephone pad—an apartment or home split—leave	bogus—bad, disgusting dog—treat someone badly posse—a group of friends skate—to avoid obligations

FIGURE 1.1: Slang terms of the past eighty years show examples of sound play and incongruity.

The word *booshwash* has an appeal largely because of the sound. The word *posse* amuses us because of the incongruous juxtaposition of that Old West image with a group of contemporary teens. Although such words might not evoke laughter, they amuse us for much the same reason that jokes do. These words also appeal to adolescents because they use irony, one of the common strategies for creating humor. This ironic code, this linguistic misdirection, immediately divides listeners or readers into two groups: insiders and outsiders—those who get it, and those who don't. In so doing, slang marks group membership, and one of the functions of youth slang is to distinguish generational groups. In this sense, slang may have two targets: an explicit one, as in the person being described as a "pill," and an implied one, which for youth slang is largely the world of adults.

- ➢ As a class project, create a slang dictionary for your own school. What's new? What's on the way out? What's the funniest? (UCLA's linguistics department has students create a college version every few years.)
- ➢ Create new slang terms. See if you can get the words to catch on throughout the school.

Jargon

While youth slang is inherently generational, dividing young from old, such creative language use is common among many distinct groups. Athletes, musicians, office workers, soldiers, and others all create a more specific kind of slang, something we might call an informal *jargon* that is connected directly to a specific profession or activity. For example, mountain bikers might use the phrase "brain bucket" to refer to a helmet, or truckers might refer to a tailgating vehicle as a "bumper sticker." Here, too, this jargon helps a group solidify a sense of identity and figuratively describe the world around them. *Wired Magazine*, a publication dedicated to new electronic technology, runs a column titled "Jargon Watch" that focuses on the slang generated by people working with new technology. For example, such words and phrases as

> beepilepsy—the brief seizure people sometimes suffer when their beepers go off, especially in vibrator mode. Characterized by physical spasms, goofy facial expressions, and stopping speech in mid-sentence.
>
> crash test dummies—those of us who pay for unstable, not-ready-for-prime-time software marketed by greedy computer companies. ("Jargon Watch")

could only have been created in the past thirty years and are a direct response to human interaction with machines. We find these terms humorous because of the wordplay (sound-alike puns) and the incongruous combination of two words or two images. Given that most students are immersed in electronic technology, this kind of slang is ripe for exploration.

- ➢ Make a list of any jargon words you have heard, especially humorous ones.
- ➢ Brainstorm ways in which current technology influences you, looking for the odd or humorous aspects of it. Then create five new humorous terms to describe that aspect of your experience with technology.

Students might also identify any other groups to which they belong and explore the jargon of those groups.

- ➢ Create a jargon chart for one or more of the following specialized areas:

  basketball band drama debate

Portmanteaus

In *Through the Looking-Glass*, Carroll uses the term *portmanteau* to describe the mixing of the sound of two words to form a new word that contains the meanings of both original words. He makes ample use of such word combinations in his poem "Jabberwocky," in which the word *slithy*, for example, is a combination of both "slimy" and "lithe." Such portmanteaus occasionally make their way into popular usage, as with the words *brunch* (breakfast/lunch), *liger* (lion/tiger offspring), and *motel* (motor/hotel).

➢ Try combining words from column 1 with words from column 2 (in any order) to see what new words you can create. Start with either word, and feel free to remove some letters if that helps to make the new word sound better.

Column 1	**Column 2**
artsy	movie
romance	book
good	luck
lunch	fast
gym	joke
evil	bad
math	principal

Comedian Rich Hall made a name for himself by creating new words that he called "sniglets" (sometimes smashing two words together to make one new one, sometimes just tweaking a word) in order to describe unusual events or things that he felt needed a name. For example, in *The Big Book of New American Humor*, Hall suggests the following as necessary additions to the English language:

> Disconfect (dis Kon fekt) v. To sterilize the piece of candy you dropped on the floor by blowing on it, somehow assuming this will "remove" all the germs.
>
> Elbonics (el bon iks) n. The actions of two people maneuvering for one armrest in a movie theater. (qtd. in Novak and Waldoks 51)

In the first instance, Hall has combined the words *disinfect* and *confection* to create a word that refers to both simultaneously. In the second instance, he has added the suffix *–ic*, which normally would transform a word into an adjective, but in this case is used more like the *–ic* in *phonics* to create a new noun pertaining to elbow usage. As you can see, there's no real restriction on how words might be coined, as long as they work.

The website *Addictionary* continues this practice, keeping a growing list of terms such as these:

> indecisijig—*noun*, the little dance that happens when you meet a stranger head-on walking the opposite direction and there is indecision about who passes on which side.
>
> shopdrifter—*noun*, a person who takes an item off the shelf in a grocery store, then later decides not to purchase it and places it on some random shelf elsewhere in the store.

The *Addictionary* site also gives readers the opportunity to contribute their own word suggestions for review and possible inclusion. Students could try working with sniglets in class or online.

- ➢ Create a class addictionary or sniglet collection.
- ➢ Contribute directly to the *Addictionary* word challenge at www.addictionary.org. (Note: as with most online dictionaries, the entries range from G- to R-rated, so some discretion is advised.)

Puns

The *pun* is a form of humor that plays off the ambiguity created when two potential meanings of the same word compete within a sentence. Although Samuel Johnson may have found the pun to be "the lowest form of humour," many great writers have used them, and most students enjoy them (at least I think their groaning at my puns is a form of appreciation). Puns rely on words with similar sounds, or *homonyms*. Normally, we would define homonym as a word with the same pronunciation as another word, but possessing a different meaning, origin, and often spelling. However, distinguishing between the following can lead to a greater appreciation of the variety of ways to construct puns:

> *homographs*—words that have the same spelling but are different in meaning, origin, and sometimes pronunciation.
>
> One brother fished for *bass* while the other plucked his *bass*.
>
> *homophones*—words that sound alike but have different meanings, origins, and sometimes spellings.
>
> You were *sweet* to rent us the *suite*.

Some words are both homophones and homographs: She went to *check* on whether her *check* had cleared the bank. And then there is a third type:

homonoids—words that have a similar sound, different spellings, and different meanings.

Faced with a challenging *baroque* recital, the musician decided to go for *broke*.

Students can work with each of these three types of word patterns.

➢ Using the chart below, construct a humorous sentence or combination of sentences based on the ambiguity of *one* of the homographs.

abuse	buffet	desert	mean	row
address	check	discard	minute	separate
ally	close	dove	present	sow
ax	concert	dress	read	spring
bank	conflict	fan	real	tear
bass	crane	lie	record	use
bed	court	live	refuse	wind
bow	cut	lose	reservations	wound

Examples:

Being in politics is just like playing golf—you are trapped in one bad lie after another.

After receiving a call from the boss telling him to quit for the night, the employee told the other clerks, "That was a close call."

➢ Using the chart below, construct a humorous sentence or combination of sentences based on the ambiguity between a *pair* of homophones.

allowed — aloud	dear — deer	mail — male	sole — soul
base — bass	grease — Greece	meat — meet	stair — stare
blew — blue	hair — hare	pear — pair	steal — steel
break — brake	loan — lone	pie — pi	waist — waste
cell — sell	made — maid	right — write	weak — week

(Note: only one of the paired words is likely to appear in the sentence; the other is implied.)

Examples:

> For this activity, the students should work in pairs, or apples if you'd prefer.
>
> If you divide the circumference of a pumpkin by its diameter, you get pumpkin pi.

➢ Take a famous phrase, and then consider homonoid half-rhymes that might replace the key words in the phrase. Create a sentence or combination of sentences that set up the pun in the altered phrase. For example, take the phrase "goes from bad to worse" and consider possible homonoid substitutes for the key words. For *bad* we might substitute *bed* or *cad*. For *worse* we might substitute *hearse* or *verse*. Substitute one, or both, words to create a new saying. Then write a lead-in that will set up that new phrase.

- The poet who writes first thing every morning goes from bed to verse.
- The evil man who insults Lara Croft often goes from cad to hearse.

Rather than focus on the types of homonyms, a different approach to puns is to explore multi-meaning words associated with a single topic. For example, words that have more than one possible meaning related to the English classroom might include *workshop, PowerPoint, rules, conventions, elements,* and *character*. From such words, comic sentences that play off multiple meanings can then be constructed: "I used a PowerPoint in my speech—darn near poked the eye out of a kid in the front row." Such an activity prompts students to associate metaphorically and think in divergent ways to uncover multiple possibilities.

➢ Create a list of multi-meaning words associated with each of the following:

baseball   band   drama   school rules

Write humorous sentences that at first suggest one possible meaning for one of the words on your list, then twist the reader toward a second definition.

One of the most common sources for unintentionally funny puns is newspaper headlines. Because headlines try to condense language, removing much of the context and modifiers necessary for unambiguous understanding, they frequently leave readers wondering about multiple meanings. For example, in the headline "Squad Helps Dog Bite Victim," there are two possible meanings: (1) the paramedics are attending to the injuries of a person who was attacked by a dog, or (2) the paramedics are assisting the dog in its attempts to bite the victim. The humor of this headline revolves around the pun in the word *bite,* which can be either a noun, as in the first meaning, or a verb, as in the second. Here are some other examples:

Police Begin Campaign to Run Down Jaywalkers

Iraqi Head Seeks Arms

Red Tape Holds Up Bridge

- ➢ Browse headlines from local papers. How many potential puns can you find? (The sports page often offers the ripest pickings.)
- ➢ Skim through a recent paper and look for an article that relies on a multi-meaning word, or think of one that might apply. Create a punning headline for that article.

One last source for puns is the advertisement. The writers of ad slogans employ a variety of strategies, including rhyme, coined words, figurative language, and occasionally puns. Some of the puns within the slogans are general and could apply to any similar company.

Security company: *Alarmed? You should be.*

Telephone company: *Technology the world calls on.*

Some puns are "branded," or integrated directly into the company or specific product name so that the slogan can apply to only one company.

Kodak Gold film: *Is your film as good as Gold?*

John Deere tractor: *Nothing Runs Like a Deere*

- ➢ Create one general pun and one branded pun for one or more products that you use.

Oronyms

We can extend our exploration of puns by adding the concept of *oronyms*, word combinations that sound the same, especially in the rush of normal speech, but have different meanings.

ice cream—I scream

Ice cream is a delicious dessert.

I scream for a delicious dessert.

mature—much your

I'm not sure how mature students will like that film.

I'm not sure how much your students will like that film.

Oronyms are a favorite strategy, along with simpler puns, of knock-knock jokes. For example, the name Norma Lee sounds much like the word *normally*, allowing for this joke:

> Knock knock! Who's there? Norma Lee. Norma Lee who? Normally I wouldn't bother you, but I need a cup of sugar.

➢ Create a couple of knock-knock jokes that include an oronym.

If students want a more difficult challenge, they might try writing a short poem or narrative in oronym form. Examples can be found in numerous places on the Internet. Do a Web search for "Eye Halve a Spelling Chequer" and "Laddle Rat Rotten Hut."

Eye Halve a Spelling Chequer	**Laddle Rat Rotten Hut**
Eye halve a spelling chequer It came with my pea sea It plainly marques four my revue Miss steaks eye kin knot sea [...] *(Sauce unknown)*	Wants pawn term, dare worsted ladle gull hoe lift wetter murder inner ladle cordage, honor itch offer lodge, dock, florist. Disk ladle gull orphan worry putty ladle rat cluck wetter ladle rat hut, an fur disk raisin pimple colder Ladle Rat Rotten Hut [...] H. L. Chace

Mondegreens

Related to the oronym is the *mondegreen*—the misinterpretation of a poem or song lyrics arising from mishearing. Sylvia Wright coined the term in a 1954 *Harper's Magazine* column to describe her frustration when she discovered her own mishearing of a line of poetry as a child. For years, she had thought these were the last two lines of the Scottish ballad "The Bonny Earl of Murray":

> They ha'e slain the Earl of Murray,
> And the Lady Mondegreen.

when in fact the lines were these:

> They ha'e slain the Earl of Murray,
> And they laid him on the Green.

Experiencing a mondegreen is common to almost everyone who listens to contemporary music. Here are a few common examples:

> I'll never leave your pizza burning (a mishearing of "I'll never be your beast of burden" sung by the Rolling Stones).
>
> Excuse me while I kiss this guy (a mishearing of "Excuse me while I kiss the sky," sung by Jimi Hendrix).
>
> There's a bathroom on the right (a mishearing of "There's a bad moon on the rise," sung by Creedence Clearwater Revival).

➢ Make a list of any mondegreens you've personally experienced when listening to music.

➢ Look at the lyrics of several pop songs and search for possible oronyms with which to "create" a mondegreen.

Daffynitions

The process by which we intentionally create oronyms or unintentionally create mondegreens leads us directly to the *daffynition,* which can be defined as the punning definition of what a word sounds like. In many cases, this means treating a single word as if it were a portmanteau. Here are a few example daffynitions:

dandelion—a well-dressed large cat

relief—what trees do in the spring

stalemate—an old spouse

porcupine—a craving for bacon

➢ Create daffynitions for each of the following words.

avoidable boycott buccaneer	eyedropper paradox protein	handicap selfish syntax

➢ Brainstorm a list of words that sound like they could be portmanteaus.

➢ Create daffynitions for each of those words.

Grammar and Conventions Humor

Metaphorical Verbs

In *Comedy Writing Secrets,* Melvin Helitzer recommends engaging writers in "association" brainstorms as kind of mental warm-up (82). For one such activity, give students a character in terms of profession—firefighter, police officer, dog catcher, gardener—and then ask them to brainstorm as many verbal adjectives as they can that might metaphorically describe a physical or psychological condition of that person. For example, in describing how a firefighter might feel coming home from work, one might list *burned up, torched, fired up, steaming,* and *not too hot,* while a similar list for a gardener might include such terms as *hosed, potted, bushed, seedy,* and *all wet.*

➢ Brainstorm similar lists for the following professions:

- police officer
- teacher
- student
- surgeon

Students can also approach *metaphorical verbs* by exploring the various ways we use animals and objects to describe the actions of people. For example, a child can "rocket around the house" or "canter" or "dart."

- ➢ Brainstorm a list of verbs based on objects or animals.
- ➢ Create some new ones, using each in a sentence that explains the meaning of the verb in context. For example:
    - Millie podded her way through school, seldom taking the earbuds out in class.
    - Joe slothed into the chair and slowly drifted off to sleep.

Metaphorical Adjectives

As with many verbs, some adjectives are inherently metaphorical, making a connection between the noun being described and some animal or thing. For example, in the sentence, "The piggish boy rooted through the dessert tray," we understand that the boy has the appetite and table manners of a pig. Authors use such *metaphorical adjectives* to create a comic tension between the two images. If you'd like to help students develop a bit of vocabulary in relation to this activity, you might point out that we have more "scientific" adjectives for most animals (see *The Phrase Finder* at www.phrases.org.uk/animal-adjectives.html for a list). For example, we could replace *piggish* with *porcine,* though the comic effect is more subtle, perhaps slightly more mature.

- ➢ Brainstorm a list of possible animal-related adjectives that could be used to describe a person. (Look up "scientific" equivalents.)
- ➢ Create new animal-based adjectives that might be useful in describing a person. Use these new adjectives in a sentence that reveals the meaning in context. (For example, "He was battish, seldom coming out of his dark bedroom except at night.")

Metaphorical Adverbs

We can also use adverbs to generate metaphorical tension in a description of a person's actions. Here, too, animals are a major contributor, as in the sentence, "She walked sheepishly into the classroom." Because we use them so frequently, such adverbs don't generate much tension anymore. However, students could examine the lists they created for adjectives (old and new) and generate some fresh *metaphorical adverbs* from them: "He burrowed molishly into the mess of his room."

➢ Create new animal adverbs.

For fun, students can explore the use of *Tom Swifties*, a term used to describe a dialogue tag such as "said" that is modified by an adverb that creates a pun out of some aspect of the dialogue, as in the following:

> I hate exams," Tom said *test*ily.
>
> "I just love Roman architecture," Tom said *arch*ly.
>
> "This canoe is leaking," Tom said *bale*fully.

Although such adverb use is a bit over the top even for most humor writing situations, it does provide an intriguing mental challenge.

➢ Create half a dozen sentences that incorporate Tom Swifties.

Though they most typically pun through an adverb, Tom Swifties can also involve a punning verb:

> "I think I'm dying," Tom croaked.
>
> "Get your cat off me," she hissed.

Students can explore this variation in conjunction with the adverb exercise, or extend the exploration of metaphorical verbs (see previous discussion) with a few of these funny dialogue tags.

Incongruous Word Pairs

Some words just don't seem to belong together, violating either our sense of logic or our sense of how syntax should work, and the resulting tension puzzles and amuses the listener. Writers most often make use of such *incongruous pairings* to create either logical incongruity—that joke went over like a *lead balloon*—or the intriguing sounds and unstable meanings generated by unusual syntax, as when two (or even three) nouns follow each other in a sentence. An example is Allen Ginsberg's use of the phrase "hydrogen jukebox" in his poem "Howl" (11, line 50). The playful aspect of such incongruous words also makes this a common strategy in the naming of rock bands, such as Led Zeppelin, Blind Melon, and Asphalt Ballet. Check out the page "Make Band Names" on the Band Name Maker website (www.bandnamemaker.com) and use the "Band Name Generator," which will give random word combinations or allow you to provide one word to which it then responds. For example, I provided "grammar," and the site returned the intriguing combinations of "grammar thunder" and "grammar casket." Have students try this activity:

- Brainstorm incongruous word pairs.
- Define these phrases (or ones created by "Band Name Generator"). Just what might "grammar casket" mean?

Ambiguous Pronouns

As with most words that have unstable meanings, pronouns can lead to humorous confusion. A vague or *ambiguous pronoun* reference occurs when there is uncertainty about which previous noun, or antecedent, a pronoun indicates. Usually such vagueness is merely a little confusing, as in the sentence, "Joe asked Bill to bring his brother to the game." In this case, "his" could refer to either Joe or Bill. Occasionally, though, such ambiguity creates a humorous moment when the wrong noun is suddenly implicated in an inappropriate action or condition:

> After the boys got out of their cars, the girls hosed *them* down.
>
> John kicked the soccer ball off the back of an opponent's head *which* rolled into the goal for a score.

Because ambiguous pronoun use is a rather common student writing error, such humorous examples can be used for corrective purposes. But the challenge of intentionally creating such errors for the sake of humor is also a great way to supplement learning how to apply the rules for pronouns and antecedents.

- Create humorous sentences by making ambiguous connections between at least two or more antecedent nouns and such pronouns as *he, she, they, them, it, that,* and *which.*

Mixing Direct and Indirect Objects

For our purposes, we'll define a *direct object* as a noun or pronoun (or a noun phrase or clause) upon which the action of a verb is directed. For example, in the sentence, "He poured *lemonade,*" the lemonade receives the action of the verb. On the other hand, an *indirect object* generally precedes the direct object and informs us to whom or for whom the action of the verb is done, as in the sentence, "He poured *Jane* lemonade." In some cases, when we mix up or leave out the direct object, we wind up with a humorous, inappropriate action. For example, if we leave out the direct object and add another action, we might get "He poured and served Jane."

- ➢ Combine the following sentences while leaving out the first direct object:
  - The cowgirl roped the bull. The cowgirl thrilled the audience.
  - The teachers cooked pancakes. The teachers served the students.
- ➢ Create several sentences that make the indirect object the inappropriate direct object of a verb's action.

Misplaced Modifiers

Simply put, a *misplaced modifier* is a word, phrase, or dependent clause that has been inappropriately separated from the noun it is supposed to modify in a sentence that has more than one noun. As with ambiguous pronouns, misplaced modifiers can frequently lead to humorous connections between the modifying description and the wrong noun. These mistakes can take many forms, but we'll focus on two types that also connect easily to instruction on how to develop details in a sentence.

The Participle

Sentences containing participles or participial phrases are prone to misplacement errors. A *participle* is a verbal, either present tense ending in *–ing* or past tense ending in *–ed* or an irregular past tense form, that acts as an adjective. For example, in the sentence, "Joe watched fireworks *exploding,*" the word *exploding* works as an adjective modifying *fireworks*. A participial phrase begins with such a verbal and is followed by some combination of other modifiers and complements, as in "Joe watched the fireworks *exploding in a colorful display*." Potentially humorous problems arise, however, whenever such a phrase is moved in the sentence so that it is closer to a noun that is not the one it is supposed to modify.

Exploding in a colorful display, Joe watched the fireworks.

We can only hope the people sitting next to Joe weren't hurt when he exploded. Past participial phrases work just as well:

Wrapped with pretty paper and tied with a bow, Mike handed her the gift.

She'd better appreciate his efforts to look good.

An exploration of misplaced participial phrases might easily follow a lesson on how to use such phrases to develop details in sentences. As with other "grammar humor," understanding the correct use is generally a prerequisite for intentional misuse. To that end, first ask students to correctly combine the following sentences:

My mother watched the factory smoke stack.

The factory smoke stack was belching fire and smoking to the heavens.

Here is the resulting combination:

My mother watched the factory smoke stack *belching fire and smoking to the heavens*.

Then have the students move the describing phrases to the front of the sentence to see what happens:

Belching fire and smoking to the heavens, my mother watched the factory smoke stack.

Once students have a sense of how to correctly add participial phrases and understand the effects of doing it wrong, they are ready to try intentionally creating a few.

> ➢ Write a sentence with two nouns, and add a participial phrase to modify the last noun in the sentence. Next, move the participial phrase to the front of the sentence so that it modifies the wrong noun.

The more absurd or silly the crossed descriptions, the funnier the mistake.

The Absolute

A second type of frequently misplaced modifier is the *absolute*, a phrase usually consisting of a noun and a modifier of that noun. In its correct position, an absolute offers a deeper description of a noun. For example, in the sentence, "Sirens howling and lights flashing, the ambulance raced to the hospital," the two absolutes (*sirens howling, lights flashing*) modify the noun (*ambulance*), giving the reader a more complete image. However, when misplaced, absolutes can create an incongruous picture:

Their tails twitching, their claws flashing, the boys tormented the cats.

His nose bulbous and red, his face pasty white, the principal watched the clown perform at the assembly.

As with the misplacement of participial phrases, an exploration of misplaced absolutes might accompany a lesson on how to use absolutes to develop details in sentences. Here, too, sentence combining might be a good place to start:

The burglar faced the dog.

The dog's fur was ruffled.

The dog's teeth were bared.

These sentences can be combined to make one:

The burglar faced the dog, *fur ruffled, teeth bared*.

Having combined the sentences correctly, students can then play with the consequences of misplacement:

Fur ruffled, teeth bared, the burglar faced the dog.

From here, students can try this activity:

➢ Generate a sentence containing two nouns, and add an absolute to further describe one of the nouns. Move the absolute so it now appears to modify the other noun.

Malaprops

A *malaprop* occurs whenever someone substitutes an inappropriate, yet similar-sounding word for another in a sentence. Coined from the French, the phrase *mal á propos*—meaning "badly suited"—appears early in English literature in the speech of many Shakespearean characters (Dogberry, Bottom, Elbow, and others) and in the character of Mrs. Malaprop (with whom the term originated) in Richard Sheridan's *The Rivals*. See the Wikipedia page "Malapropism" for numerous examples of literary, film, and pop culture malaprops, including these:

> "Our watch, sir, have indeed *comprehended* two *auspicious* persons." (that is, *apprehended, suspicious*) —*Much Ado about Nothing*, Act 3, Scene V
>
> "I am not going to make a *skeptical* out of my boxing career." (that is, *spectacle*) —Tonya Harding
>
> "The *ironing* is delicious." (that is, *irony*) —Bart Simpson after finding Lisa in detention.
>
> "I'm so smart it's almost scary. I guess I'm a child *progeny*." (that is, *prodigy*) —Calvin, to which Hobbes replies, "Most children are."

Another source of such malaprops is students, as linguist and teacher Richard Lederer has documented in several books, such as *Anguished English*, which includes these examples:

> "The Puritans thought every event significant because it was a massage from God." (7)
>
> "A triangle which has an angle of 135 degrees is called an obscene triangle." (5)

The easiest way to create malaprops is to begin with two sound-alike words or phrases and then construct a sentence that allows the misuse of one of them.

> indomitable—abominable: The abominable explorer sailed westward.
>
> acute—a cute: He had a cute appendicitis.
>
> gorge—garage: He had a double-car gorge with a blue door.

As with grammar humor, creating intentional mistakes generally requires that one know the correct usage. In this case, malaprops can be a humorous way to liven up a vocabulary study when employed in the traditional way of having students use their vocabulary words in a sentence.

➢ Brainstorm sound-alike words or phrases for a few words in your vocabulary list. Create malaprop sentences using the wrong word in place of the correct vocabulary word.

Typos

Akin to malaprops, but generated from a different kind of error, is the humorous *typo*. Most typographical errors result in the creation of misspelled words that are not funny. Occasionally, however, typos result in meanings that are radically altered from what was originally intended: "He told the police that one of them menaced him with a wench while the other covered him with a revolver." The distinction between a typo and a malaprop is one of degree—a malaprop might be quite different in spelling from the word intended, but a typo is usually off by only one letter. In addition, malaprops are typically spoken by a character, but typos are necessarily written. As a result, typos tend to work best when associated with such things as official reports, advertisements, menus, newsletters, and the like.

➢ Brainstorm a list of items that might be included on a school lunch menu. Consider which ones might be altered with a one-letter typo. Create a humorous typo for a school menu item.

➢ Look at some magazine advertisements, and make a list of the words used. Consider which ones might be altered with a typo. Revise the advertisement for humorous effect.

Jokes

The Rule of Three

One of the most common strategies for creating jokes is the *rule of three*. The writer creates a list or series of three ideas or things: the first sets the theme, the second confirms it, and the third twists it into a moment of surprise. Film director and comedian Woody Allen uses the rule of three frequently. A passage complaining about the narrator's declining health sets up the reader with "My room is damp and I have perpetual chills and palpitations of the heart," and then the narrator surprises the reader with "I noticed, too, that I am out of napkins. Will it never stop?" (227) Sherman Alexie is fond of using this strategy for a kind of dark comic effect. In his poem "Father Coming Home," Alexie describes the father as "carrying the black metal lunch box with maybe half a sandwich, maybe the last drink of good coffee out of the thermos, maybe the last bite of a dream" (*Business* 63), surprising us with the last phrase.

The three items can be single words—"He was my dream date: *tall, dark,* and *dumb*"—short phrases, or complete sentences. In *The Comic Tool Box,* John Vorhaus recommends an activity in which student writers complete the sentence starter "Three things you should (never) . . ." by listing two expected answers and following those with a truly unexpected answer (105). For example:

> Three things you should never say to your English teacher:
>
> "I don't have a pen."
>
> "This book is boring."
>
> "Is that your hair, or is a porcupine on your head?"

Recognizing the value of such surprises and practicing this technique in a variety of forms will allow students to work unexpected humor into their own writing.

- ➢ Create a sentence, reviewing a movie you've seen, that uses a series of single words, the first two setting a pattern of expectation, and the third word humorously violating it.
- ➢ Create a series of three sentences, describing yourself, with the first two following a logical pattern, and the third undercutting that pattern.

Reversals

A standard element of many jokes, the *reversal* takes a recognizable character type or situation, gives the audience just enough to set up expectations, and then violates those expectations with a contradictory conclusion. For example, we're all familiar with the stories that older people often tell about how maturity and experience has helped them understand the world in a more thoughtful way.

When Oscar Wilde says, "When I was young, I thought that money was the most important thing in life. Now that I'm old—I know it is," he depends on our familiarity with this situation and sets reader expectations for a lesson in wisdom. But the last four words of his statement reverse that expectation.

Because jokes or witty statements are usually quite short, the author or speaker does not have much time to evoke expectations. As a result, these jokes tend to rely on people, things, or events that are easily recognized in just a few words. This is one of the reasons we see categories of humor such as doctor jokes or mother-in-law jokes or cat jokes or jokes about football or baseball. Each of these categories relies on a stereotypical knowledge of the subject. Notice how the following joke depends on our previous knowledge of the character type, and how the expectations from that knowledge are reversed in the end.

> "I told my psychiatrist that everyone hates me. He said I was being ridiculous—everyone hasn't met me yet." —Rodney Dangerfield

The joke is funny precisely because a flippant and hostile response is so incongruous with our perception of psychiatrists and how they communicate with their patients.

Similar expectations can be evoked by common events with which we are familiar. Comedian Steve Martin sets up this punning joke with a picture of a loving pet owner:

> I gave my cat a bath the other day. They love it. He just sat there and enjoyed it. It was fun for me. The fur kept sticking to my tongue, but other than that . . . (49)

The reversal here is all the more effective because it not only disrupts our expectations of bathing a pet, but does so by switching the speaker's traits with the cat.

Students can ease into this technique with a couple of prompts:

➢ Complete the following with statements that reverse the expectations.

- I went to a high school football game. It was really violent. You should have seen . . .
- My English teacher is a real stickler for rules . . .
- I said to my school counselor, "I'm having difficulty concentrating on my schoolwork." She said, . . .

Then students can create expectations on their own:

> ➢ Create several reversal jokes by first providing a recognizable setup and then following it with a reverse.
>
> Setup: ____
>
> Reverse: ____

Misdirection

Similar to reversal, *misdirection* involves deliberately misleading the reader into thinking a sentence or paragraph is heading in one direction, and then quickly changing direction to surprise the reader. Typically, misdirection begins with easily recognizable kinds of texts—clichés, famous or everyday documents, popular song lyrics, or even joke standards. For example, consider this joke:

> Three men walk into a bar; you'd think one of them would have seen it.

Here, the humor relies on the reader recognizing the standard "walk into a bar" joke form. This sets up an anticipated direction, which presumably involves going into a bar and having a conversation with the bartender or other patrons. The misdirection of this joke hinges on the pun on the word *bar*. Yet this is only revealed in the second part of the joke, which now places the men on a sidewalk, or at a construction site, but probably not in a place where they can order drinks. (For a good visual example of misdirection, see the many *Calvin and Hobbes* comics that begin with Calvin as Spaceman Spiff or the detective Tracer Bullet, only to end up with Calvin in his seat in class or being chased by his mother.)

Although students can create misdirection jokes out of any quickly recognizable text, the easiest way to give them practice is to explore clichés. Normally, clichés are the bane of student essays, and we struggle to help students recognize why including such overused phrases weakens their writing. The following activity attempts to turn the negative into a positive, showing students how to transform clichés into effective humorous moments. The problem with clichés is that there is no moment of surprise or freshness, so we need to alter the cliché in such a way that it ends with a surprise.

> ➢ Find a cliché or short aphorism:
>
> If at first you don't succeed, try, try again.

> ➢ Then brainstorm alternative endings that will surprise the reader. W. C. Fields offered this: "If at first you don't succeed, *then quit. There's no sense being a fool about it.*"

The surprise ending might replace part of the cliché, or it might follow:

> "What goes up, must come down, *but don't expect it to come down where you can find it.*" —Lily Tomlin

And students might find it easier if they add the word *if* at the beginning of the cliché to help set up the surprise:

> "If all the world's a stage, *it's time to change the director*." —Russell Goebel

Have your students brainstorm some common clichés and aphorisms, or search for clichés at *Cliche Finder* (www.westegg.com/cliche) and give them new life.

Non Sequitur

There are two kinds of *non sequiturs*—logical and literary. In logic, a non sequitur is a conclusion that does not follow two or more premises that are assumed to be true. Usually these premises are not particularly funny. For example, a detective might note that the murderer used a pair of scissors as a weapon, and the professor owned a pair of scissors; therefore, the professor is the murderer. Whether or not the conclusion is true, it doesn't really follow from the two premises provided and certainly wouldn't stand up in a court. Occasionally, seemingly logical non sequiturs can be amusing: "God is love. Love is blind. Ray Charles is blind. Therefore, Ray Charles is God" ("Ray Charles").

Most humorous non sequiturs, though, are of the literary type and tend to be absurd conclusions or interruptions in a kind of story logic. Misdirection might suggest that a joke is headed in one direction, and then the joke takes us in another; one form of literary non sequitur might suggest a direction, only to lead us into a nonsensical dead end. For example:

> How many surrealists does it take to screw in a light bulb? Giraffe.

A more common type of literary non sequitur involves the insertion of a comment that is completely out of context, with a bit of dialogue or stream of thought. If, during the interrogation of our hapless, murdering professor, the detective says,

"We know you own a pair of scissors, so you might as well confess. And, by the way, did you know there's a great sale today at Macy's?"

the reader will likely be surprised by the seemingly random insertion of shopping. Students might play with literary non sequiturs through the following:

- ➢ Take a standard joke and give it a non sequitur punch line.
- ➢ Create a short piece of dialogue in which one of the characters keeps inserting seemingly random comments.

You might also point out that visual non sequiturs are common in humorous films. For example, in *Blazing Saddles,* as the bad guys are galloping their horses across a desert of scrub and sage brush, they are suddenly delayed by a tollbooth that requires dimes.

Exaggeration

Humor that intensifies some aspect of a character or a condition relies not so much on incongruity for its effect as on distortion. Writers look for a distinctive physical trait, a behavior, a manner of speech, and then exaggerate it so that, like a fun-house mirror, the distortion makes us laugh. Think of the way that political cartoons take one physical feature—Bill Clinton's chin or George W. Bush's ears—and stretch it to the limits of recognition. Of all the humor strategies covered in this chapter, *exaggeration* carries with it the greatest potential for hostile critique. Exaggeration is at the root of most ethnic and gender humor (whether oppressive or subversive) and revels in stereotypes that can be amplified. Such humor is usually too risky for a secondary classroom, even if the study of such humor can reveal a great deal about the history of racism, sexism, ableism, and other prejudices. So we'll place some boundaries on our exploration.

In general, exaggeration tends to focus on physical qualities, abilities, or some event or condition, most often emphasizing the negative. Given that negative humor about other people is often offensive, let's look at a few alternatives that make this safer for the classroom. First, we might limit ourselves to self-deprecating humor, keeping ourselves as the target. For example:

Physical quality: "I was skinny. I'd turn sideways and disappear."
—Sherman Alexie

Ability: I was such a bad student that in middle school I flunked lunch.

Condition: "There were thirteen kids in my family. We were so poor we had to eat cereal with a fork, so we could pass the milk to the next kid." —Bernie Mac

Before pursuing this activity, be sure students understand that the jokes don't need to have anything to do with their real selves. They are simply using "I" as a target because that's relatively safe. If it helps, they can imagine a fictional character who is speaking.

➢ Create three self-deprecating exaggerations about a physical trait.

➢ Create three self-deprecating exaggerations about incompetence in some area.

(Note: if students need help getting started, suggest that they begin with phrases such as "I'm so __ that . . ." or "I'm so bad at ___ that . . .")

Alternatively, students can pick a safe external target, such as cats or dogs.

Physical quality: My dog's breath is so bad, it knocks squirrels out of trees.

Ability: My cat is so lazy that she hires other cats to nap for her.

➢ Create two exaggerations about a pet's physical qualities.

➢ Create two exaggerations about a pet's abilities.

Exaggerating about things, conditions, or events is usually a bit safer than focusing on personal qualities, because no one person or group is necessarily targeted. Instead, a writer chooses a recognizable moment or thing and distorts its effect. For example, "That band was so bad that even the cockroaches left the building."

➢ Create an exaggerated negative response to one of the following:

basketball game	homework	pep rally	school hallway
bus ride	lecture	pop song	school lunch
field trip	movie	school dance	school play

Of course, exaggeration can focus on the positive; unfortunately, we simply don't find positive distortions nearly as funny as negative ones. But that in itself can be the challenge. Students can repeat the previous activities while emphasizing some positive aspect: "I'm so handsome that . . ." "My dog's so smart that . . ." "The band was so good that . . ." Or you might challenge them to a kind of reverse "dozens" contest.

> ➢ With a partner, take turns trying to top one another's exaggerations in response to some version of the following: My mama's so smart that . . .

Top Ten Lists

One comic form of joke with which nearly all students are already familiar is the *top ten list*. This list is really a series of one-liner jokes based on the same theme, usually using exaggeration or irony as humor strategies. David Letterman has made this a staple of the *Late Show*. Here's how one begins:

> **Top Ten Signs You're Watching a Bad Monster Movie**
> 10. Monster comes to New York, takes in a matinee of "Jersey Boys" and leaves.
> 9. He doesn't eat people—he just licks them. [. . .]
> (For the rest of this list and many others, see the *Late Show* Top Ten Archive online at http://lateshow.cbs.com/latenight/lateshow/top_ten /archive.)

Notice how such a list also relies on surprise by offering answers that oppose our normal expectations. In other words, we have to know what makes a good monster movie and understand the monster film genre in order to get the jokes. In this sense, the challenge for student writers is to know the topic well and then to think in opposites with a bit of exaggeration.

Laurie Halse Anderson uses a slightly different version of this comic strategy in her novel *Speak*, by having the traumatized main character, Melinda, point out some of the essential ironies of high school life:

> The First Ten Lies They Tell You in High School
> 1. We are here to help you.
> 2. You will have enough time to get to your class before the bell rings.
> 3. The dress code will be enforced. [. . .] (5–6)

In this list, the humorous surprise depends on the reader recognizing incongruity between the school's claims and students' actual experiences.

By being selective about the *topic*, a teacher can turn this into an interpretive activity or an examination of high school culture or an exploration of national politics.

➢ Create top ten lists for the following:
  - Top Ten Signs the Old Man Has Been Out to Sea Too Long
  - Top Ten Things You Should Never Do at a High School Dance
  - Top Ten Ways You Know Your Member of Congress Is Making Promises that Won't Be Kept

For a change of pace, students might want to try their hands at humorous multiple-choice questions that follow essentially the same format, with the question providing the topic, and the four answers providing the humor.

Comic Definitions

Unlike daffynitions that intentionally misinterpret a word for comic effect, *comic definitions* take the word at face value, but offer a humorous interpretation of its standard meaning. Ambrose Bierce popularized this kind of comic definition in his 1911 book *The Devil's Dictionary*, in which he offered numerous explanations of terms, particularly about politics, social mores, and religion, which were frequently more "accurate" than one would find in a typical dictionary.[1] For example, he skewers both the right and the left in the following:

> CONSERVATIVE, n. A statesman who is enamored of existing evils, as distinguished from the Liberal, who wishes to replace them with others.

In some ways, Bierce was a precursor to the NCTE (National Council of Teachers of English) Doublespeak Award, in that he revealed the ways in which people use language to mask their real intentions. This is one of the reasons that Bierce's approach to defining terms, and the approach of his many imitators, is often called *cynical lexicography*. This gives us a clue as to how to go about creating such definitions. One strategy is to assume the worst in ourselves and others (it's just an exercise, not a lifestyle recommendation) and then interpret a term with the idea that someone has something to hide. For example, consider the following definitions:

> ADMIRATION, n. Our polite recognition of another's resemblance to ourselves.
> APOLOGIZE, v.i. To lay the foundation for a future offence.
> EGOTIST, n. A person of low taste, more interested in himself than in me.

Bierce skews each definition to point out the psychological rationalizing that we seldom admit. A second approach, especially with terms about professions or types of people, is to identify a strength and exaggerate it into a weakness, as Bierce does in the following:

> HISTORIAN, n. A broad-gauge gossip.
> LAWYER, n. One skilled in circumvention of the law.

Most terms can be explained in such a cynically humorous way, but students might find the task most interesting if they have the opportunity to define the terms pertaining to school life.

➢ Create an *Imp's Dictionary* that uses humorous, school-based definitions for the following terms:

school	teacher	school lunch	date	cell phone
art	student	locker	boyfriend	football
math	principal	pep rally	girlfriend	soccer
science	counselor	dance	music	band
English	vice principal	fire alarm	textbook	backpack

Captions

Creating *captions* for photographs is another great way to practice creative thinking and apply a variety of humor strategies. Photos of pets can work particularly well, though if you visit the *I Can Haz Cheez Burger* website (http://icanhascheezburger.com), you'll see examples of humorous captions to photos sorted in categories of cats, dogs, celebrities, news, sports, and others. The photos themselves don't have to be funny. For example, look at the image of a kitten in Figure 1.2. It's cute, but not funny. However, if we caption it by giving surprising thoughts to the cat, we can use the photo as a means

FIGURE 1.2.

FIGURE 1.3.

toward humor. The first step is to imagine what a slightly personified cat might be thinking in this situation. Then find a humorous way to give voice to those thoughts, as shown in Figure 1.3.

The following captions all use the same photo for a different joke.

> More catnip?
>
> Oh, no . . . claws stuck. Help!
>
> Today the scratching post . . . tomorrow the curtains.

Notice how each of these exaggerates a different personality type that we might associate with the kitten—from scared to gluttonous to helpless to mischievous.

➢ Bring in two or three photos of your pets (or pick some animal photos from *National Geographic*). Working in small groups, generate several captions for each of the photos.

Note

1. Although Bierce's dictionary is largely classroom appropriate, it does contain some of the ethnic slurs common in its day. In addition, many of the definitions are heavily ironic and satiric. Student readers should understand that Bierce is not advocating, but rather describing what he sees as corrupt perspectives and behaviors in his society.

2

Funny Stories and Essays

What I like best is a book that's at least funny once in a while.

—THE CATCHER IN THE RYE, *J. D. Salinger*

Despite the fact that many great writers—William Shakespeare, Jonathan Swift, Jane Austen, Mark Twain, Langston Hughes, to name a few—devoted much of their artistic focus to humorous stories and essays even while addressing serious issues, reading lists in secondary classrooms seldom incorporate texts that are funny. For those who choose the books that students must read, there is clearly something attractive about tragedy and complexity. There is an unwritten literary rule that, whether exploring the Trojan War or World War II, the plight of peasants under tyrannical rule or the plight of African Americans under slavery, struggles with disability or struggles with patriarchy, great wisdom can come only from readers vicariously experiencing great pain. This may in part be true, but only if the reader is receptive.

Unfortunately, this focus on the tragic often does not match the reading interests of students, especially those we are most trying to reach. Poet and novelist Paul Beatty recounts, in the introduction to *Hokum*, his negative response as an eighth grader to a literary "gift" from the Los Angeles school district:

> For a black child like myself who was impoverished every other week while waiting for his mother's bimonthly paydays, giving me a copy of *I Know Why the Caged Bird Sings* was the educational equivalent of giving the prairie Indians blankets laced with smallpox or putting saltpeter in a sailor's soup. I already knew why the caged bird sings, but after three pages of that book I now know why they put a mirror in the parakeet's cage, so he can wallow in his own misery. After this traumatic experience I retreated to my room to self-medicate with Clavell, Irving,

> Wambaugh, the Green Lantern, Archie and Jughead: it would be ten years before I would touch another book written by an African-American. (7–8)

Beatty confirms what Michael Smith and Jeffrey Wilhelm point out in their book *"Reading Don't Fix No Chevys"*: many students simply find such tragic and serious texts uninteresting, and will offer a variety of resistance strategies when asked to read them. Smith and Wilhelm suggest that one way to ease students into reading and discussions of serious issues is to do so through a framework of humor, both in terms of text selection and activities related to reading. They propose that humorous texts are effective for helping students "explore various critical lenses to understand social issues, for providing students the opportunity to talk back and make fun of authors and texts through comedy routines, for simply using humor to engage them with ideas [. . .] Our data encourage us to have more fun with our students and read more material that is humorous" (196–97).

Extending this argument for selecting humorous texts to engage students as readers, I suggest that giving students the opportunity to *write* humorous stories and essays may well have an encouraging effect on students as writers. I suspect that one of the challenges adolescents face in writing is that we ask them to strip their prose of real "voice" even while saying that we *want* voice. In other words, most students feel that the expectations for academic writing require an approximation of the dry style of an encyclopedia, a voice far removed from their own experience. While there is certainly a value in learning to sound "serious," there is also a value in being true to one's own voice. We know it helps immensely to "write what you know," and what many students know is the often comic world of adolescents, their decidedly rich vernacular, and a sarcastic wit. Whether in the form of fiction, memoir, or essay, humor writing can allow students to speak naturally about what they know well.

Elements of Humorous Stories

In the face of state writing tests that demand improvement in expository and persuasive writing, narrative writing has lost much of the standing it once had in the secondary English classroom. This is a shame because telling stories is one of the fundamental aspects of human life, and telling funny stories can get one dates. But, as with all forms of humor, comic stories require a specific set of skills; they require an understanding of how to create comic characters, conflict, plot, and point of view, and how to apply humor strategies in a more extended fashion.

Before we look at each of these elements in turn, a quick word about topics for humor writing. Personal experiences are wonderful sources for funny stories. However, it's important for students to understand that there is a distinction between a funny moment—the time Dad's turkey exploded on Thanksgiving, or when my brother got his head stuck between the stairway banister rails—and a funny, well-developed story.

> ➢ Brainstorm a list of funny moments with family or friends, choose one, and write a paragraph describing the moment in careful detail.

After they have had the opportunity to share these, ask students if these are "stories." Ideally, students will recognize that the paragraphs lack many of the fundamental aspects of stories, especially conflict and plot. They are, instead, vignettes—short, descriptive literary sketches or "photographs" of a moment in time. Funny stories typically have several such vignettes within them, linked by conflict and plot.

The important thing for students to understand is that funny stories need characters with goals, and conflicts or obstacles that frustrate those goals. So those are the things we'll explore in some depth.

Characters

Most humorous fiction relies heavily on comic *characters*. We might begin our examination of character by simply asking students to brainstorm what makes a character funny. The list they create will likely be diverse and unwieldy, but if asked what most of the attributes they listed have in common, students may recognize that most comic characters tend toward narrow, extreme personalities. In other words, for these characters, a single personality trait tends to dominate their words and behavior. Because of this, most comic characters easily fall into recognizable categories. For example, in *The Eight Characters of Comedy*, Scott Sedita suggests that nearly all television sitcoms recycle the following comic character types:

- The Logical Smart One
- The Lovable Loser
- The Neurotic
- The Dumb One
- The Mean One

- The Womanizer / Manizer
- The Materialistic One
- In Their Own Universe (49)

Each of these types of characters offers a different range of joke possibilities. For this reason, most sitcoms and most humorous stories utilize two or more of these types to broaden the story line options. Let's look at an example from a popular television show. Of the six main characters in the sitcom *Friends*, three fit well into this template. Joey is "the dumb one," Phoebe is clearly in her own universe, and Monica is an obsessive-compulsive neurotic. The other three characters are a bit more complex, yet can still be associated with these types: Ross is also a neurotic, Chandler a loveable loser (with just a bit of sarcastic meanness), and Rachel a materialist. Regardless of the plot of individual episodes, much of the humor of *Friends* is generated by the characters' representations of these types.

> ➢ Examine a sitcom of your choice and write a brief explanation of how the characters might fit into these categories.

Such comic character types are not limited to sitcoms, but populate films and literature as well, and even show up in genres that we would not label as comedy. For example, although the original *Star Wars* is an action-adventure film, the function of the neurotic robot C-3PO is almost entirely for comic relief in an otherwise tension-filled story line.

In young adult (YA) literature and film, these categories still apply, though they tend to be blended with the stereotypical cliques that we associate with middle and high school culture—groups such as jocks, preps, stoners, and nerds. In many cases, these groups are seen through a lens of those comic categories: the nerd is logical to a fault, the preppie is a materialist, the jock is the mean one, the stoner is the dumb one. Of course, in real life, such stereotypes fail to capture the complexity of human experience—which is the whole point of such films as *The Breakfast Club*. Nevertheless, these groups are still ripe comedic territory.

> ➢ In small groups, choose a popular teen sitcom or film comedy, and then prepare a brief presentation on how the comic types mix and match with the stereotypical YA groups.
>
> ➢ Create four or five characters that blend comic types with YA stereotypes. For each character,

- list personality traits that might emerge from the stereotype (these should be at least a little extreme);
- describe the kinds of clothes the character wears that match the stereotype;
- list the character's favorite words or phrases when speaking—language stereotypical of his or her group;
- predict the kinds of conflicts such a character would likely encounter.

Then continue the exploration:

➢ Just to keep things flexible, create a character that violates the comic type or stereotype connection. In addition, brainstorm how this violation might serve as a source of comic conflict. How, for example, might an extremely logical and literal jock create tension in a room of stereotypical athletes or in a conversation with a coach?

> "All right you guys, I want you to get tough and go out there and crush them like bugs!"
>
> "Uh, coach. I'd like to point out murder is illegal and is hardly sporting. Besides, we'd need to be approximately 7.3 times as large as they are to have the leverage necessary to crush a human body."

If you find a reliance on comic types a bit too restricting, character creation can be made more flexible by simply focusing on character flaws. In *The Comic Toolbox,* Vorhaus offers several quick prewriting suggestions for creating humorous stories in relation to comic characters and conflicts. To create comic characters, he suggests that the writer needs to determine four things:

1. a character's *comic perspective*—the primary motivation or desire that drives the character
2. a character's *flaws*—the behavioral or personality traits that create problems for the character
3. the *exaggerated outcome* of those flaws—types of conflicts or problems created by the flaws
4. a character's "*humanity*"—the internal part of the character that makes us care (42)

So, for example, we might create a protagonist with the following outline:

- Character: John Cando
- Comic perspective: *believes he can improve everything*
- Flaws: *overconfidence, lack of real skills*
- Exaggeration: *makes wildly impulsive mistakes due to overconfidence*
- Humanity: *well meaning*

From just this brief description, we can anticipate how such a character might respond to other characters and to conflicts that might arise. A character who wants to improve the world, who wants to make a big splash and leave his mark, is going to make certain choices that, say, a slacker character whose primary motivation is to "just chill" simply won't make. His overconfidence will lead him to tackle goals and projects beyond his grasp. His lack of real skills will virtually guarantee failure at those tasks. Despite this, his real sense of meaning well will allow the reader to feel for him, which intensifies the emotional response to the humor.

When students have generated a number of possible comic characters, ask them to reflect on possible names for them. While most authors tend to use "normal" names, which is perfectly fine, some authors prefer to ham it up a bit—from Charles Dickens with Gradgrind and Pecksniff, to Joseph Heller with Major Major Major, or the many goofy names in the Harry Potter series. In many comic stories, names can play an important role in quickly creating character. For example, in Patrick McManus's quasi-autobiographical stories, his best friend is Retch and his dog's name is Strange. In Anderson's *Speak*, the protagonist refers to two teachers as Mr. Neck and Hairwoman. In all of these cases, the character names are indicative of personality.

➢ Brainstorm a list of possible humorous names for one of your characters. For example, which of the following might best describe a male jock who is mean? Logical? Neurotic? A womanizer?

Max Looker	Jacque Mann	Joe Dulstuump
Jim Shu	Mick Swagger	Stu Tistics
Jim Shorts	Stone Kyler	Ben Rules

In creating character names, puns, nicknames, portmanteaus, and odd spellings are all welcome.

You could extend this exploration of character creation through names by having students brainstorm funny team mascot names and odd school clubs to which characters might belong. Why, for example, might J. K. Rowling have chosen the name Slytherin for one of the Hogwarts houses? What does the name sound like? What does it imply about anyone who is a member of this house and his or her potential flaws? Anderson similarly uses this strategy for comic effect in *Speak,* as Melinda reflects on the possible misuses of such mascots as Hornets and Trojans, and briefly allies herself with the Marthas, a group dedicated to emulating Martha Stewart's fashion and decorative flair. Bierce, in his book *The Devil's Dictionary,* uses group names to satirize and characterize all types of people. Despite being one hundred years old, these odd group names still resonate today and can serve as models. For example:

Ancient Order of Modern Troglodytes

Blatherood of Insufferable Stuff

Cooperative Association of Breaking into the Spotlight

Genteel Society of Expurgated Hoodlums

League of Holy Humbug

➢ Generate humorous names for the kinds of groups that teens, parents, teachers, and other possible characters might belong to or be labeled as.

Conflict

Once students have settled on a character, they can begin exploring possible comic moments and *conflicts*. Whether they have created a comic character from one of the types or through a more specific fault, they will need to consider what kinds of conflicts and challenges their character would most likely encounter. For example, if they chose a materialist, what conditions might best bring out the character's comic nature? What setting and conflict might put the most pressure on him or her? In other words, if a rich, pampered, unintentionally snobby (but still likeable) character is comfortable in a world of Beverly Hills or Manhattan parties, what happens if she is marooned in the wilderness? Imagine if Brian in Gary Paulsen's rugged survival story *Hatchet* had instead been Cher from the film *Clueless,* or that Cher had been on the plane with Brian. What kinds of comic moments could arise in relation to such topics as clothes, food, sleeping accommodations, hygiene, makeup, and hair?

Or, if we take the example of John Cando, who is overconfident and incompetent but wanting to improve things, in what context and under what conditions would such a character encounter or create the most problems? If he were a new recruit in the army, Cando might decide to help the general by tricking out his jeep with rocket engines; or if he were the student manager of the basketball team, he might rig the players' shoes with springs. In any case, the character's perspective and desires should be frustrated, and his flaws should lead to temporary comic disasters.

For an abbreviated version of this relationship between character flaws and humorous conflict, see the comic strip *Foxtrot*. Each character in the strip has distinct flaws and an ongoing set of conflicts that arise from them:

> Peter believes he is great at sports but isn't, great at driving but isn't; he is also a procrastinator, a glutton, and overly concerned with looking manly.
>
> Jason is arrogantly intelligent, cluelessly geeky, grossly incompetent at all things physical, and obsessed with video games.
>
> Paige is materialistic, vain, and obsessed with boys.
>
> Roger is technologically challenged and incompetent at most household tasks.
>
> Andy is a health-food nut and an overly careful money saver.

From each of these flaws, a variety of conflicts arise on a regular basis.

➢ Read some *Foxtrot* comic strips (widely available on the Internet and in book form) and fill out the following chart.

Character	Flaws	Conflicts
Jason		
Peter		
Paige		
Roger		
Andy		

➢ Create a similar chart for your comic characters and their flaws and likely conflicts.

Plot

Humorous short stories generally follow the traditional story arc, moving from initial conflict to rising tension to climax and resolution, yet there is often a unique *plot* pattern to comic fiction within this arc. In his *Comedy Writing Workbook*, writer Gene Perret refers to this as a "plus – minus" sequence that permeates short stories, sitcoms, and films. The idea here is that comedy generally (though not always) relies on the initial failure of the protagonist. She makes a plan. The plan ends badly. Yet she manages to turn the failure into a positive or at least get back to where she started. Adapting an activity from Perret (170–73), I suggest the following sequence to help students think through this pattern:

1. Begin with a simple problem and a character's plan to resolve it.
2. Next, brainstorm possible worst-case scenarios, and then choose the most comically promising.
3. Resolve that scenario, and turn it into something seemingly positive (or at least neutral).
4. Next, complicate that solution by having it lead to another worst-case scenario.
5. Resolve this scenario, and again turn it to a positive.

Let's look at a quick outline example. Returning to John Cando, the ambitious, overconfident, but generally incompetent character, we'll place him in the following scenario:

1. He wants to treat his girlfriend to the most romantic, lavish prom date ever, but he doesn't have the money. He decides to enter a talent contest that has a first prize of $500, but he doesn't tell his girlfriend because he wants the prom date to be a surprise. (This is our initial plus.)

2. While playing Sting's romantic song "My One and Only Love," his voice cracks, and he makes mistakes throughout the song, beginning with the very first lines where, instead of saying, "The thought of you makes my heart sing," he says, "The thought of you makes my heart sting." The audience laughs, and he walks off humiliated. (This is our first minus.)

3. Afterward, several friends who saw the show congratulate him on being so funny. So he decides to try to get a job doing musical comedy. He finds a coffee shop that will pay him $50 to perform. (Our second plus.)

4. Unknown to him, his girlfriend walks in while he is performing and hears him sing the line "The thought of you makes my heart sting." She thinks he's making fun of her and storms off. (Our second minus.)

5. He takes his guitar, stands under her window, and plays and sings the original song beautifully. She comes to the window. He tells her what he's been doing for the prom. She's touched, they reunite, and she tells him that she'd rather spend a quiet evening with him than go to prom anyway. (This is our resolution.)

Alternatively, you might help students develop a comic plot by having them fill out the graphic organizer in Figure 2.1 based on what Vorhaus calls a "comic throughline" (76–77).

Who is the protagonist?	
What does the protagonist want?	
The door opens.	
The protagonist takes control.	
A monkey wrench is thrown.	
Things fall apart.	
The protagonist hits bottom.	
The protagonist risks all.	
What does the protagonist get?	

FIGURE 2.1: This organizer shows the development of a comic plot.

Given that the stories that most middle and high school students write are likely to be fairly short (500 to 2,000 words), one or two plus-minus scenes or a quick comic throughline are probably all they will be able to adequately explore.

> ➢ Using the plus-minus pattern or Vorhaus's graphic organizer, create a plot outline for your story.

While the students have been developing characters and conflict to lead to plot, you might want to point out that it's possible to work backward at this story development. To illustrate this, you can have students revisit their brainstormed list of funny experiences (remember my dad's exploding turkey) and think about how those moments might be part of this character intention, flaw, and conflict equation. If we want this humorous moment to be the climax of our story, what kind of character and conflict might lead to it? For example, how might we set up Dad's intention and flaws so they might logically lead to an exploding turkey? Whether true or not, let's say Dad is overconfident and a bit of a chauvinist. (A discussion of the comic license to alter and distort for laughs might be in order here.) Let's say that after Mom asked to go out for Thanksgiving dinner, Dad told her she was being a baby, that it's easy to cook such a meal. In fact, he'd do it better than she ever did. Let's say Mom bets him a month's worth of laundry if he can pull it off. All of which sets up the story arc that leads to the explosion. In this way, students can take their comic memories, which they know in rich detail, and transform them into brief, fictional stories.

> ➢ Create a story outline that plausibly leads to your chosen humorous memory.

If students struggle to come up with story ideas, you might point out that when it comes to a basic plot, originality is not altogether necessary. There are very few new ideas in humorous stories. How many comic conflicts, in print and on television, have been made of the boy trying to avoid showing his report card to his parents? Or the girl whose fashion choice backfires? Or the boy or girl who risks embarrassment to get the boy or girl of his or her dreams? Shakespeare borrowed comic ideas from Boccaccio; the writers of *10 Things I Hate About You* borrowed ideas from Shakespeare. Yet, while plot ideas may be borrowed, modified, and recycled (within copyright boundaries, of course), the humorous new way in which the story is told is what counts.

➢ Brainstorm a list of common humorous stories, and then make a list of ways that you might make one of these stories new.

Point of View

Humorous fiction can be told equally well from either a third-person or first-person *point of view*, but it's crucial that the point of view helps to quickly reveal the protagonist's or the narrator's perspective on life through his or her desires, and his or her flaws. This generally requires extended access to a character's thoughts or a revelation of narrator bias. Let's look at the first few paragraphs of three different short stories to get a sense of how this might work, beginning with the third-person limited omniscient point of view in "The Secret Life of Walter Mitty." James Thurber begins the story with what appears to be a straightforward adventure sequence:

> "We're going through!" The Commander's voice was like thin ice breaking. He wore his full-dress uniform, with the heavily braided white cap pulled down rakishly over one cold gray eye. "We can't make it, sir. It's spoiling for a hurricane, if you ask me." (55)

The rest of the introductory paragraph details the commander's bravery in flying a "hurtling eight-engined Navy hydroplane" through dangerous weather. So far, however, this is not funny at all. But then the second paragraph begins,

> "Not so fast! You're driving too fast!" said Mrs. Mitty. "What are you driving so fast for?"
>
> "Hmm?" said Walter Mitty. He looked at his wife, in the seat beside him, with shocked astonishment. (55)

In just the first three paragraphs, Thurber has revealed his protagonist's dreams (to live an exciting life) and his flaws (passivity, daydreaming, timidity). The humor of this piece is generated primarily from two things: (1) the misdirection of action stories dissolving into a domestic one, but more important, (2) the conflict between the character's desires, how he "acts" on those desires by dreaming, and the repeated failure of that action to change his condition. Notice that a degree of omniscience was necessary for the reader to understand. Without access to Walter's thoughts, none of the humor would have been possible.

A first-person point of view makes this internal access more immediate. For example, in the Jack Handey short story "The Voices in My Head," the narrator/protagonist offers his own self-analysis:

> I never know when the voices in my head are going to start talking to me. I might be coming out of my apartment and I'll look up at the clouds. Suddenly, the voices in my head will tell me to go back inside and get an umbrella, because it might rain. Sometimes I'll obey the voices and go get the umbrella. But sometimes I muster my strength and refuse to get the umbrella. Still, the voices don't let you forget that you disobeyed them, especially if it rains. They'll say, "I knew you should have gotten the umbrella. Why didn't you?"
>
> I don't expect you to understand what it's like to have voices in your head telling you what to do. But it is a nightmare I live with all the time. Right now, for instance, the voices are telling me to go back and change the word "nightmare" to "living hell." (85)

Like Walter Mitty, the protagonist here might be categorized as an "in his own universe" type of comedic character. But this is apparent only by access to his thoughts, which reveal his belief that his rational thinking is somehow separate from his own personality. From the very first paragraph, the reader can see that the protagonist desires, not unlike many adolescents, to be left alone and not told what to do. His flaw is in extending this desire in an exaggerated fashion to his own conscience.

It is possible to generate humor in a third-person point of view without showing character thoughts, but this generally requires revealing the bias of the narrator. For example, in Twain's "The Story of the Bad Little Boy," the narrator's desires are implicitly revealed very early:

> Once there was a bad little boy whose name was Jim—though, if you will notice, you will find that bad little boys are nearly always called James in your Sunday-school books. It was strange, but still it was true, that this one was called Jim.
>
> He didn't have any sick mother either—a sick mother who was pious and had the consumption, and would be glad to lie down in the grave and be at rest but for the strong love she bore her boy, and the anxiety she felt that the world might be harsh and cold towards him when she was gone. Most bad boys in the Sunday-books are named James, and have sick mothers, who teach them to say, "Now, I lay me down," etc., and sing them to sleep with sweet, plaintive voices, and then kiss them good-night, and kneel down by the bedside and weep. But it was different with this fellow. He was named Jim, and there wasn't anything the matter with his mother—no consumption, nor anything of that kind. She was rather stout than otherwise, and she was not pious; moreover, she was not anxious on Jim's account. She said if he were to break his neck it wouldn't be much loss. She always spanked Jim to sleep, and she never kissed him good-night; on the contrary, she boxed his ears when she was ready to leave him.

Stripped of the narrator's attitude and observations, this is, so far, a story about a boy who has an uncaring and abusive mother. Not a particularly funny topic. But in the very first sentences, the narrator makes clear his bias (that Sunday-school books are unrealistic) and his desire (to entice the listener to agree, by offering incongruous juxtapositions of religious fantasy and harsh reality). In a way, the narrator creates a comic character out of the religious fantasy, a character who is continually frustrated in making his ideals real. And all of this takes on even more comic tension if one is aware of Twain's own battles with censors and his disdain for the hack Sunday-school writing that often outsold his own.

All of which is to say that in humor writing, point of view plays a special role, one that sets up the possible ways to reveal crucial aspects of comic characters. As a rule, first person tends to be a bit easier, and it allows for the development of an internal voice of the narrator that is so crucial to the humor of much young adult literature. Novels such as *Speak*, *The Catcher in the Rye*, and *The Absolutely True Diary of a Part-Time Indian* all rely heavily on first-person internal monologue for the funny, sarcastic observations of society in general and school cultures in particular.

➢ Reflect on the difference that point of view might make in your story. Which point of view seems the most promising? Why?

Applying Humor Strategies

Once students have outlined their characters, conflict, and plot, and selected a point of view, they're ready to begin drafting the story. Now the real fun starts. While the basic story elements set up a framework for a comic story, the humor is generated by the careful application of basic humor strategies. But a word of caution is in order. Unlike in stand-up comedy, humor in stories and essays generally requires a more subtle approach than just telling jokes (though those are still occasionally possible in dialogue and in character thoughts). In a story, the writer has more time to develop and lead into a humorous moment. More important, stories require sustained attention on the part of the reader—the longer the story, the more this is true. And one of the keys to sustaining a reader's attention is to find a balance between being funny and advancing the story's plot. In addition, given that humor relies on surprise, there have to be moments of calm in order to set up the surprise moments. Or, as S. J. Perelman notes, "When you endeavor to be funny in every line you place an intolerable burden not only on yourself but on the reader. You have to allow the reader to breathe" (qtd. in Schreiber 53).

Skunk Dog

When I was a kid, I used to beg my mother to get me a dog.

"You've got a dog," she would say.

"No, I mean a real dog," I'd reply.

"Why, you've got Strange, and he's a real dog, *more or less*."

Strange was mostly less. He had stopped by to cadge a free meal off of us one day and found the pickings so easy he decided to stay on. He lived with us for ten years, although, as my grandmother used to say, *it seemed like centuries*. In all those years, he displayed not one socially redeeming quality. *If dogs were films, he'd have been X-rated.*

I recall one Sunday when my mother had invited the new parish priest to dinner. Our dining room table was situated in front of a large window overlooking the front yard. During the first course, Strange passed by the window not once but twice, walking on his front legs *but dragging his rear over the grass. His mouth in an ear-to-ear grin of sublime relief, and possibly pride in his discovery of a new treatment for embarrassing itch.*

"Well, Father," Mom said in a hasty effort at distraction, "and how do you like our little town by now?

"Hunh?" the pastor said, a fork full of salad *frozen in mid-stroke as he gaped out the window at the disgusting spectacle.* "Pardon me, what were you saying?" (18–19)

If students aren't quite sure what this means, you might offer them the following analogy. They are watching a horror movie, and suddenly a monster pops out and starts chasing the protagonist. While the protagonist is running, another monster pops out and joins the chase. And then another and another and another . . . Although viewers might have jumped in surprise when the first monster popped out, and may have jumped a little when the second one appeared, they likely won't respond much to the subsequent monsters. In fact, no matter how scary the monsters might be, this scenario would get rather boring after a while. That's why horror films tend to follow a pattern of encounter—escape—rest—encounter—escape—rest so that each appearance of a monster is a fresh surprise. A similar idea applies to using humor elements in stories.

Let's look at an example (at left) from the beginning of a McManus story, "Skunk Dog." I've marked the humorous elements with italics.

The "jokes" in this piece come at a fast clip, but even so, McManus gives time for the reader to stop smiling before hitting her with the next joke. Notice that there are three-and-a-half "straight" sentences before the first sarcastic "more or less" that clues us in to the humorous trajectory of the piece. This is followed by two-and-a-half more sentences that aren't funny, but which set up context for the exaggeration in "it seemed like centuries." This is followed by another setup sentence that precedes the funny film comparison. Then the author gives us another two sentences of description, which set up the dog's slapstick behavior. Then a sentence to break the humor, followed by another visual joke in the shocked pastor. Even at this rapid pace, the humorous elements are broken up by several sentences that offer description and push the plot forward. In less frenetic humorous stories, there might be only two or three humorous elements per page.

With this pattern of setup and then surprise in mind, let's look at the humor strategies common in funny stories. Chapter 1 addressed a wide variety of humor strategies (from puns to jargon to jokes), most of which can find their way into a short story in one form or another, but students can really create effective humor by just relying on three basics—exaggeration, slapstick, and irony.

Exaggeration

Exaggeration is the mainstay of most humorous stories. It's a strategy that seems to come naturally to adolescent writers and works well from a first-person point of view. Alexie sprinkles exaggeration throughout his novel *The Absolutely True Diary of a Part-Time Indian*, with the first few pages containing such self-deprecating comments by the protagonist, Arnold, as these:

> "I was skinny. I'd turn sideways and disappear." (3)
>
> "My head was so big that little Indian skulls orbited around it." (3)
>
> "Everybody on the rez calls me a retard about twice a day." (4)

In his book *Rock This*, Chris Rock uses exaggeration to make fun of the stereotypical assumptions many people make about African American men.

> All black men are born suspects. When I came out of my mother, right away, if anything happened within a three-block radius, I was a suspect. As a matter of fact, the day I was born, somebody's car got stolen from the hospital parking lot. They made me stand in a lineup. That was pretty tough, considering I wasn't even a day old and couldn't crawl, much less walk. Good thing I had a couple of black nurses to help hold me up. I got lucky. They were in the lineup too. (8–9)

These bits of exaggeration not only add humor to serious, sensitive topics, but also tell us something about the personality of the narrator.

Remember, too, that metaphor and simile often function in the form of exaggeration. For example, in Ron Koertge's *Stoner and Spaz*, the protagonist describes the theater owner's teeth: "Reginald grins, showing me what looks like part of the keyboard of a tiny, decaying piano" (3).

- ➢ List exaggerations common in everyday speech and in your school.
- ➢ Create several exaggerating similes and metaphors to describe a school lunch, a stereotypical politician, or a football game.
- ➢ Write one-sentence exaggerations that describe the characters or the setting of your story.

Sometimes, students may want to explore a more extended form of exaggeration. In another McManus story, "My First Deer, and Welcome to It," the narrator reflects on the tendency of hunters to, well, exaggerate. In the following passage he uses exaggeration to describe how his friend Retch's first deer, which was "only slightly larger than a bread box," grew over time.

> Not long ago, Retch and I were chatting with some of the boys down at Kelly's Bar and Grill and the talk turned to first deer. It was disgusting. I can stand maudlin sentimentality as well as the next fellow, but I have my limits. Some of those first deer had a mastery of escape routines that would have put Houdini to shame. Most of them were so smart there was some question in my mind as to whether the hunter had bagged a deer or a Rhodes Scholar. I wanted to ask them if they had tagged their buck or awarded it a Phi Beta Kappa key. And big! There wasn't a deer there who couldn't have cradled a baby grand piano in its rack. Finally, it was Retch's turn, and between waves of nausea I wondered whether that little spike buck had developed enough over the years to meet this kind of competition. I needn't have wondered.
>
> Retch's deer no longer walked in typical deer fashion; it "ghosted" about through the trees like an apparition. When it galloped, though, the sound was "like thunder rolling through the hills." And so help me, "fire flickered in its eyes." Its tracks looked like they had been excavated with a backhoe, they were that big. Smart? That deer could have taught field tactics at West Point. Retch's little spike buck had come a long way baby. (55)

Notice how closely related this kind of *extended exaggeration* is to that used in traditional American tall tales. Notice, too, how the core of the exaggerated tall tale is present in teen films such as *Ferris Bueller's Day Off*, where the protagonist progresses from accomplishing the merely improbable to becoming nearly god-like at the climax of the story.

- ➢ Write a brief scene in which a character is bragging or dreaming about his or her exploits with progressively bigger, more preposterous exaggerations.
- ➢ Consider whether an extended exaggeration might work in your story.

Slapstick

Young adults have a penchant for *slapstick* humor. Physical comedy that ends in someone's embarrassment clearly resonates with an age group fearful of embarrassment. This is an element of humor that students know well already, so use their knowledge to start off this brief investigation.

- ➢ Brainstorm favorite (appropriate) slapstick moments from films, television, and the Internet.

Most likely, students will list a preponderance of scenes from shows like *America's Funniest Home Videos* or from *FailBlog*: random scenes of a dad pitching a ball to a toddler, only to have the little one hit the ball into Dad's groin; or a clip of a skater trying to jump a set of stairs, only to fly into the person shooting the video. Be sure to nudge students beyond the random, and ask them to include scenes from film comedies and television sitcoms.

- ➢ After you've made a substantial list, separate the slapstick moments into two categories:

  1. Moments that are funny out of context of a story

  2. Moments that contribute to the development of character, conflict, or plot

(Note: some moments might do both.)

For examples of moments that contribute to the plot or characterization in a story, the continuous physical missteps of Inspector Clouseau in *The Pink Panther* contribute to and extend from his character. And in *The Breakfast Club*, the scene where the vice principal turns to leave the library, revealing a trail of toilet paper emerging from the back of his pants, contributes to the film's overall challenging of false notions of authority.

This distinction between *incidental* slapstick and *integrated* slapstick is important because in a short story, there is no room for any scenes that don't contribute to the development of character, conflict, and plot. In other words, students need to understand that in humorous stories, the slapstick must serve a specific purpose, not just be tossed in for laughs. (Though it might be fun to have a funniest slapstick paragraph contest.)

In his often funny, yet ultimately sad and reflective novel *Looking for Alaska*, John Green makes use of slapstick moments to tell us something about characters; for example, when the protagonist Miles (Pudge) first meets the character Alaska, who has just finished telling an amusing story to Miles and his roommate (the Colonel) about getting her boob "honked" (another bit of slapstick, actually). The story Alaska tells doesn't really sink in to Miles because he is so immediately enamored of this beautiful, intellectual girl.

> "Who's the guy not laughing at my very funny story?" she asked.
>
> "Oh, right. Alaska, this is Pudge. Pudge memorizes people's last words. Pudge, this is Alaska. She got her boob honked over the summer." She walked over to me with her hand extended, then made a quick move downward at the last moment and pulled my shorts down.
>
> "Those are the biggest shorts in the state of Alabama!"
>
> "I like them baggy," I said, embarrassed, and pulled them up. They had been cool back in Florida. (15)

Apart from just being funny in a high school sort of way, this quick bit of slapstick serves a specific function in that it tells the reader to always expect the unexpected from Alaska.

In the story about Dad and the Thanksgiving Day disaster, a slapstick paragraph such as the following might serve as the climax:

> All eyes turned to the golden-browned turkey as it began to hiss. The skin began to tighten and swell, and a large bulge began to press out in the center, as though a chest-bursting alien were about to gnaw its way out. The ribcage swelled outward and a plume of steam began erupting from the neck cavity. With a *bang-splllattt*, the turkey exploded, raining white and dark meat down upon the table and the heads and shoulders of everyone seated there.
>
> Taking a piece of turkey off of her forehead and eating it, Mom turned to Dad and said, "Well, Hon, I think it's done."

> ➢ Consider if there are opportunities for slapstick moments in your story. Briefly explain how a specific moment would contribute to character development or advancing the plot, then write the scene.

Irony and Sarcasm

It's one of those odd coincidences that students have such difficulty reading irony in great literature (Twain's *Adventures of Huckleberry Finn*, Ralph Ellison's *Invisible Man*, George Orwell's *1984*) when they swim in irony in their everyday lives. From simple words—for example, using *sick* to mean *good*—to sarcastic phrases like "isn't she just a prom queen," adolescents are adept at saying one thing and meaning another. Luckily, this is another trait that can be put to good use in their humor writing. First, it would help to give them a couple of brief definitions. For the purposes of this chapter, these definitions will be simple, though a more in-depth exploration of irony can be found in Chapter 4.

> *irony*—a statement that says one thing but means another. (I think it's important not to use the word *opposite* in the definition because this causes confusion and is often not true.)
>
> *sarcasm*—an ironic statement that is meant to ridicule a person, action, or thing.

With these definitions in mind, have students try these activities:

> ➢ Make a list of the ironic statements most common in your experience. Place an *S* next to those that are meant to sarcastically ridicule.
>
> ➢ Consider whether any of your story characters would likely use this kind of irony or sarcasm. If so, brainstorm a few comments that he or she might make.

The kinds of ironic statements that the students list will undoubtedly be dominated by examples of *verbal irony*. These are things that people often say out loud in dialogue, or in written communication that tends to mimic speech, such as a diary, journal, email, or text message. As a result, if students want to incorporate this kind of irony in their stories, it would likely come in one of those forms. In her novel *Speak*, Anderson uses verbal irony continually in the form of Melinda's journal comments. Her "First Ten Lies They Tell You in High School" list, beginning with "We are here to help you," is all a kind of verbal irony, as are such section titles as "Our Teachers Are the Best," "Our Fearless Leader," and "Dinner Theater." All of these also qualify as sarcasm because they are meant to ridicule school and family. (Her proclivity for such biting irony would categorize Melinda as a "mean one" comedy character type, though she certainly has reason enough for this attitude.)

In addition, students should also consider *dramatic irony*, which occurs when the reader knows something that one or more of the characters do not, so as to alter the meaning of what a character says or does. Sometimes the protagonist is in on the trick with the reader. For example, when Anne (of Green Gables) apologizes to Mrs. Lynde for being insulting, the reader and Anne know, and Marilla suspects, that this is largely an exercise in dramatic performance and imagination. On the way to the apology, Anne is excited about the prospects of the performance, and once there she breaks into "character."

> Rapt and radiant Anne continued until they were in the very presence of Mrs. Lynde, who was sitting knitting by her kitchen window. Then the radiance vanished. Mournful penitence appeared on every feature. Before a word was spoken Anne suddenly went down on her knees before the astonished Mrs. Rachel and held out her hands beseechingly.
>
> "Oh, Mrs. Lynde, I am so extremely sorry," she said with a quiver in her voice. "I could never express all my sorrow, no, not if I used up a whole dictionary. You must just imagine it. I behaved terribly to you—and I've disgraced the dear friends, Matthew and Marilla, who have let me stay at Green Gables although I'm not a boy. I'm a dreadfully wicked and ungrateful girl, and I deserve to be punished and cast out by respectable people forever. It was very wicked of me to fly into a temper because you told me the truth. It *was* the truth; every word you said was true. My hair is red and I'm freckled and skinny and ugly. What I said to you was true, too, but I shouldn't have said it. Oh, Mrs. Lynde, please, please, forgive me. If you refuse it will be a lifelong sorrow on a poor little orphan girl, would you, even if she had a dreadful temper? Oh, I am sure you wouldn't. Please say you forgive me, Mrs. Lynde."
>
> Anne clasped her hands together, bowed her head, and waited for the word of judgment. (Montgomery, Chapter 10)

Without our knowledge of Anne's "performance," this text would read as just a self-abasing apology, but *with* our knowledge it reads instead as a ruse, a subtle insult to the intelligence of Mrs. Lynde, and a sign of Anne's cleverness. The judgment she really awaits is not forgiveness but applause.

In *The Catcher in the Rye*, J. D. Salinger uses a continuing strategy of allowing us to hear Holden Caulfield's thoughts, transforming his speech into irony. For example, Holden as narrator explains to the reader that Ernest Morrow is "the biggest bastard that ever went to Pencey" and "as sensitive as a goddam toilet seat," which then sets up Holden's conversation with Ernie's mother:

> "Well, a bunch of us wanted old Ernie to be president of the class. I mean he was the unanimous choice. I mean he was the only boy that could really handle the job," I said—boy, was I chucking it. "But this other boy—Harry Fencer—was elected. And the *reason* he was elected, the simple obvious reason, was because Ernie wouldn't let us nominate him. Because he was so darn shy and modest and all. He refused. . . . Boy, he's *really* shy. You oughta make him try to get over that." I looked at her. "Didn't he tell you about it?" (74)

As a result of our being in on the joke, the entire dialogue can be read as an audacious, funny lie.

> ➢ Create a brief dialogue between two characters from a first-person point of view that allows the reader to hear the thoughts of one of the characters. Have the one character's thoughts make the dialogue ironic.

If students can't think of a way that this might work in their story, just have them practice by using the scenario of one character asking another out, with the thoughts of the character being asked out revealing his or her true feelings while the dialogue suggests something else.

Sometimes, however, the protagonist is the one who is ignorant of what the reader and other characters know. In Jerome K. Jerome's wonderful Victorian comic novel *Three Men in a Boat (To Say Nothing of the Dog)*, the protagonist narrator is an "in his own universe" type of character who usually interprets events in unusual ways. This allows for a number of delightfully ironic passages. For example, he is continually convinced that he is ill, even dying, and has a proclivity for "catching" any disease he hears or reads about in books or advertising circulars.

> In the present instance, going back to the liver-pill circular, I had the symptoms, beyond all mistake, the chief among them being "a general disinclination to work of any kind."
>
> What I suffer in that way no tongue can tell. From my earliest infancy I have been a martyr to it. As a boy, the disease hardly ever left me for a day. They did not know, then, that it was my liver. Medical science was in a far less advanced state than now, and they used to put it down to laziness.

> "Why, you skulking little devil, you," they would say, "get up and do something for your living, can't you?"—not knowing, of course, that I was ill.
>
> And they didn't give me pills; they gave me clumps on the side of the head. And, strange as it may appear, those clumps on the head often cured me—for the time being. I have known one clump on the head to have more effect upon my liver, and make me feel more anxious to go straight away then and there, and do what was wanted to be done, without further loss of time, than a whole box of pills does now.
>
> You know, it often is so—those simple, old-fashioned remedies are sometimes more efficacious than all the dispensary stuff. (5)

Our knowledge of the narrator's hypochondria and his proclivity to laziness allows us to read the passage as a hilarious indicator of just how out of touch with reality he is. It's not necessary that the character be so goofy, just merely misinformed. The old Miss Litella skits on *Saturday Night Live* present a hard-of-hearing elderly commentator played by Gilda Radner, who would rail against the "Deaf Penalty" until Chevy Chase would whisper, "That's *death* penalty." Miss Litella would then say, "Hmm. That's entirely different. Nevermind" (Radner 63).

➢ Think of a scenario where a character overhears a conversation and grossly misunderstands and, as a result, ends up acting in an extreme way.

Or, if students have trouble coming up with an idea, try this:

➢ In small groups, write out a brief scene where a student character overhears one of the cafeteria staff say to another, "This poison ought to slow those little twerps down." The reader, but not the overhearing character, gets to see that this speaker is referring to cockroaches and not the student body. How might this tiny bit of dramatic irony evolve into a story? Write out the scene and then outline how this might lead to comic behavior.

Now that students have crafted characters, outlined a comic plot, and practiced applying a few basic humor strategies to fiction writing, it's time for them to draft the story. One of the great things about having students write humor is that they are all eager to read each other's work. Because the stories are generally about adolescent experience, they bring an expertise as critical reviewers to a writing workshop. And they are almost always enthusiastic in offering constructive criticism when prompted to help each other make the stories funnier.

Best of all, from a teacher's standpoint, reading a stack of funny stories is almost always more pleasant than reading a stack of five-paragraph critical essays—unless, of course, you've assigned them humorous essays instead.

The Humorous Essay

In many ways, writing humorous essays is easier than writing stories, and allows for the incorporation of more humor strategies. Stories almost always have the burden of plausibility, consistency, and story arc. Essays are much more open to experimentation, digression, and language play. The only restriction, generally, is that there be some kernel of truth to what is being said about a topic. But it can be a rather twisted truth, with no real sense of "fairness" that we might associate with the non-humorous essay.

For our purposes, let's begin with a fairly straightforward essay of just 200 to 300 words, and then we'll explore a few alternative forms. But first, let me say that what I'm about to suggest is a fragile crutch that should be used once or twice as a learning tool and then altered or discarded. It's a template to help students acclimate to one type of humorous essay, and any and all attempts to expand it or go beyond it or go around it should be encouraged once they have the general idea.

Choosing a Topic

The initial challenge that students face in writing humorous essays is choosing a topic. The truth is, almost any topic can be funny. Go to an improv theater: the actors will turn prompts like "hydrology," "stamp collecting," and "hamburgers" into hilarious skits. The trick is to see what's funny in a topic. So students should start there.

- ➢ In small groups, brainstorm a random list of things, places, and events. For example:

Things	Places	Events
computers cats couch	the beach Disneyland middle school	camping football games school dance

- ➢ Then choose one and make a list of what's funny about it, with minimal censoring or judging of the ideas.

Let's take school dances, for example. A list of what's funny about dances might include these ideas:

- People don't dance.
- People can't dance.
- Some people think they can dance, but they can't.
- Some people think dancing is "making out" to music.
- It's really a fashion show disguised as a dance.
- Chaperones are like prison guards or zoo keepers.
- Decorating a gym is like putting lipstick on a pig made of cinder blocks.

➢ After constructing a list of funny aspects, choose two or three that have the greatest potential for humorous description. Then quickly shape these into an outline. For example:

1. Introduction: Dances Are Funny Things

2. People Don't Dance

3. People Can't Dance

4. Conclusion

➢ For each body paragraph topic, create another list, one of exaggerated descriptive details, words, slang, metaphors, similes, and the like that would help illustrate in comic fashion the points you are trying to make.

For a paragraph on the idea that "people can't dance," students might list such things as these:

- Tragically arrhythmic
- Like suffering from a leg cramp
- Need cheat-notes to dance steps
- Dancing to the beat of different drummer, clearly not the one in the band
- Two left feet, one of which is completely devoid of a sense of direction
- Doing the funky chicken as if the chicken's head were cut off
- Can't manage a two-step side-to-side slide without tripping himself (or herself) and date
- Like a rhinoceros in a mosh pit

At this point, students will have developed possible "evidence" for their paragraphs. One of the pleasures of writing humorous essays is the freedom to create and distort evidence as well as find it.

Notice that the list we've just made is highly subjective and opinionated. This leads to another difference between more traditional persuasive or expository essays and humor essays: the author/narrator is nearly always present. Whether in first person or third person, the personality and attitude of the author/narrator should shine through. Much humor is generated out of the personality of the speaker, and this is true of essays as well as stand-up. Dave Barry writes his essays from a "guy's" perspective, Rita Rudner from a "woman's," and their observations take on the stereotypical perspectives of those points of view. George Carlin offers a "cynic's" view, Rock writes from a "black man's" perspective, and Ellen DeGeneres writes as a "naïve innocent." Students don't need to adopt a comic character type (though they could if they wanted), but they do need to position themselves (or a funny persona) as the voice of the essay.

With this prewriting done, let's look at introductions, a body paragraph, and conclusions.

Introductions

Introductions in humor are crucial. In traditional essays we tell students how important it is to use a "hook" or a "grabber." This is even more true in a humorous essay. The first paragraph should generate a laugh (or at least a smirk). Remind students that humor relies on surprise, so in this first paragraph they need to find a way to set up the readers for one expectation, and then jolt them with the unexpected. This can be done in a single-sentence paragraph. For example, here is one of Barry's openings that leads to an essay on Americans buying 3.5-gallon toilets in Canada to skirt a new U.S. law:

> I say it is time our "leaders" in Washington stopped blathering about sex and started paying attention to the issues that really MATTER to this nation, such as whether we should declare war on Canada. (*Dave Barry Is Not Taking* 49)

Notice how Barry uses a serious, chastising tone and emphasizes the idea of important issues, then surprises us with the absurd. Here's another example, this time leading to an essay on body image and television:

> If there's one ideal that unites all Americans, it's the belief that every single one of us, regardless of ethnic background, is fat. (*Dave Barry Is Not Taking* 168)

Here again, Barry begins with a serious tone, makes reference to American ideals, suggesting that this will lead to some topic like justice or freedom, and even emphasizes this possibility with "regardless of ethnic background." Then he ends the sentence with "is fat," jarring us in a humorous way.

If we take our topic of school dances, we could draft several possible opening lines roughly modeled after Barry's, looking for one that might best elicit a laugh and lead into the essay. For example:

1. While our school administration obsesses over state testing and makes pointless rules about dress codes and parking, they ignore really crucial high school issues, such as requiring boys to actually dance at school dances.
2. If there's one beautiful, romantic memory that lasts in the minds of all high schoolers, it's that moment at the prom when someone breaks into a funky chicken routine.

> ➢ Look at these two examples, and at the Barry examples, and underline the parts that "set up" reader expectations. Then circle the parts that disrupt those expectations.
>
> ➢ Create two opening single-sentence paragraphs for your essay that follow a similar pattern.

If students want a more developed first paragraph, say three to five sentences, they will still want to follow this pattern of setup and surprise, only this time they will have the opportunity to use the first two or three sentences for setting up the joke. Once again, here's an opening paragraph from Barry, though this one runs three sentences:

> Most Americans are pitifully ignorant of geography. This was clearly demonstrated recently when the Gallup Organization sent its pollsters to Chicago to ask randomly selected residents if they could name at least three of the six major continents. The results were shocking: Most of the pollsters never found Chicago at all; of those who did, all but one fell into the Chicago River. (*Dave Barry Is Not Taking* 75)

In this paragraph, Barry begins with a straightforward, often-heard claim about American world knowledge that could easily be the first sentence of a serious essay on the state of our education system. He follows this up with a sentence that appears to lead toward trustworthy quantitative evidence to support his claim. Then, in the third sentence, he offers up an exaggerated, absurd, and unexpected example, though it certainly does support his claim. Using this as a model, we might generate something like the following for our school dance opening:

> There is nothing so romantic as a school dance. Ask any of last year's students, and they will share memories of soft lights, slow music, and beautiful dresses. But most of all, they will tell about how the Lansky twins slam-danced across the room, knocking over seven couples, bouncing off two chaperones, upending the refreshment table, and coming to a final rest with the punch bowl balanced on their heads.

Notice that this paragraph uses slapstick as its source of humor, but that's just one of many humor strategies students might apply.

- ➢ Try a more extended first paragraph, beginning with a two-sentence setup followed by a humorous, unexpected development in the third sentence.

Body Paragraphs

Having an introductory paragraph in place, students are ready to craft a few body paragraphs. In general, these will follow a similar pattern of setup and surprise, though students should feel free to experiment with how that might take shape. For example, the sentences in a paragraph might follow an alternating pattern of setup / sentence-of-surprise, or the paragraph might offer three or four setup sentences leading into a single surprise. As with traditional essay body paragraphs, however, it's generally a good idea to begin with a topic sentence. Continuing our exploration of school dances, our two body paragraphs might look something like the following.

> This is the problem with dances; they are attended by boys with the same social graces as a pack of confused hyenas. Guys in high school are smart people. They can master AP history and calculus, repair their own cars, and even read a blitzing defense. So why, at a school dance, do they mill about on the sidelines, staring downward as if desperately searching for the cheat-notes to dance steps they have written on their shoes?
>
> As a guy myself, I'd like to say these young men are actually budding dance stars too shy to strut their stuff. I'd also like to say I look like Brad Pitt. But seriously, even the boys who get confused, take a wrong turn, and wind up on the dance

floor still don't really dance. Instead, as an article in the *Journal of Strange Male Behavior* explains, boys at dances suffer from tragic arrhythmia, spasmodic seizures, and lapses in mental judgment rendering them incapable of managing a simple side-to-side slide step without tripping themselves and their partners, and leaving them prone to breaking out into the chicken dance without any warning.

In these two body paragraphs, there is at least a sentence of setup separating each of the funny parts. The humor strategies employed are simple enough; there is a simile and two exaggerations, with the non sequitur bit about Brad Pitt tossed in. Nothing to it.

➢ Write two or three short body paragraphs for your essay, being sure to use some version of the setup / surprise pattern and several different humor strategies (exaggeration, metaphor or simile, slapstick, rule of three, misdirection, and so on).

Conclusions

With this done, students are ready to finish with a short conclusion. As with any persuasive or expository essay, finishing with a call to action or a final observation and judgment is a good idea, only once again we'll turn to the setup–surprise pattern.

So I call upon the administration to take immediate action to remedy this dance problem in the only way that will ensure that the entire student body is capable of properly getting into the groove: *make this an all-girls school.*

Next week's topic: Bare Midriffs and the War on Terror.

➢ Write a conclusion that sounds as if you are making a reasonable call to action or a commonsense observation, only to end with an outrageous or absurd suggestion.

Other Nonfiction Forms

As I mentioned earlier, the model of humorous essay that I have presented is just one of many possible approaches. It has the advantage of being simple, and is easily explained, but it should not become some kind of five-paragraph straightjacket. Variety is an important part of the comic surprise. To that end, students can also explore other nonfiction forms that lend themselves well to humor. Here are a few.

The Q & A

Perhaps the easiest is the question-and-answer format. The Q & A starts with what appear to be serious or least semi-serious questions (the setup), which are then followed by humorous answers. Even more than with humorous essays, this form benefits from the assumption of a "character of authority" for effect. This might be a doctor, a psychologist, an advice column writer, a teacher, and so on. For example, the following piece circulating on the Internet has a medical doctor being interviewed.

> The Dr. Answers Your Health Questions
> Q: I've heard that cardiovascular exercise can prolong life. Is this true?
> A: Your heart is only good for so many beats, and that's it. Don't waste them on exercise. Everything wears out eventually. Speeding up your heart will not make you live longer; that's like saying you can extend the life of your car by driving it faster. Want to live longer. Take a nap.
>
> Q: Should I cut down on meat and eat more fruits and vegetables?
> A: You must grasp logistical efficiencies. What does a cow eat? Hay and corn. And what are these? Vegetables. So, a steak is nothing more than an efficient mechanism for delivering vegetables to your system. Need grain? Eat chicken. Beef is also a good source of field grass (green leafy vegetables).
>
> Q: How can I calculate my body/fat ratio?
> A: Well, if you have a body and you have body fat, your ratio is one to one. If you have two bodies, your ratio is two to one, etc. ("Doctor's Advice")

The humor throughout this sequence rests in the misapplication of logic by a supposed authority. In this sense, we are looking at an extended form of the reversal (see Chapter 1) where the authority violates our expectations.

This same format can come in different contexts—an advice column on fashion and dating, a teacher's answers to exam review questions, a father instructing his son (see Bill Watterson's *Calvin and Hobbes* strip where the dad explains that the sun sets in Arizona, 153). The important thing is that the person answering the question is an authority of some sort.

It might be worthwhile to show students that the same humorous material can be approached in different ways by taking the school dance essay and transforming part of it into the Q & A format.

> Dr. Lara Love's Dating Advice
> Q: Dr. Love, whenever I go to a dance with my boyfriend, I'm totally embarrassed. It's like he's not even trying to dance right. What gives?
> A: Try not to blame your boyfriend. He probably can't help it. According to the *Journal of Strange Male Behavior*, boys at dances suffer from a social disease characterized by tragic arrhythmia, spasmodic seizures, and lapses in mental judgment leaving them incapable of managing a simple side-to-side slide step without tripping themselves and their partners, and leaving them prone to breaking out into the chicken dance without any warning. It's best to just park him by the punch bowl and dance with your girlfriends.

The joke is largely the same, only this time it comes in a different form and with a hint of authority and advice. Which form makes this particular topic funnier?

- Translate one piece of your essay into a Q & A format, and then self-assess the effect the form has on the humor.
- Create a Q & A interview with an authority offering surprising, humorous advice.

The Letter

We spend much of our time praising some things and complaining about others, so we might as well have a sense of humor about it and write funny letters to the people and things responsible. For example, doesn't George Lucas deserve an angry letter about the danger to viewers posed by Jar Jar Binks? Or McDonald's for its insensitive abuse of all those people afraid of clowns? Or maybe the brains behind the size chart for women's clothing deserve some derision. Claire Suddath begins her letter of complaint,

> Dear Totally Impractical Size Chart for Women's Clothing,
> I've been dealing with you for nearly 12 years, since that summer in junior high when I skyrocketed to atmospheric heights, head and shoulders above my classmates, and the clothing in the kids' section of the department store no longer fit my long legs and gangly arms. My mother took me to your side of the store, and, for a moment, I felt mature, womanly, the kind of mystical feminine that one only

> sees in movies. I was one step closer to being an adult. I was happy. And then I tried on your clothes.
>
> Everything I tried on I had to try on in threes. For years, I've been carting trilogies of skirts and pants into the dressing room, armfuls at a time, because I have no idea what size I wear. I can make an approximation, but that "size" ranges between three of your numbers, depending on the store, because these sizes don't actually mean anything. I'm an 8, but an 8 of what? Inches? Feet? Joules, the numeric value describing the relation between heat and mechanical work that I used in my high-school physics class and then never again? Is that it?

On the other hand, doesn't someone deserve praise for those vibrating, rocking, gaming chairs? Or the reinvention of 3-D movies? Or how about Taco Bell's Crunchwrap Supreme? Roxanne Paris begins her love letter to this sexy fast-food product this way:

> Hello, darling,
>
> They tried to keep us apart, but true love can never be separated for long.
>
> When I first met you, I was younger and more naive. I figured everything from Taco Bell tasted alike. They were all just variations of the same ingredients. How wrong I was. I tried you on a whim. You didn't seem like anything special. But you were new, and I was hungry. So I ordered you, oblivious to the delight you would bring to my inexperienced mouth.

Such letters allow for a personal voice and a quirky perspective to create humor out of our daily lives.

> ➢ Write a letter of complaint to a person, company, or the product itself.
>
> ➢ Write a love letter to a product.
>
> Use exaggeration, figurative language, slapstick, irony, and the other humor strategies as needed.

The Diary or Journal

The casual, disjointed form of the diary or journal make it a natural fit for a kind of running humorous commentary on an experience that takes place over time. Unlike with a short story or memoir, the writer doesn't really have to worry about a plot, but rather has the opportunity to just make humorous observations as things develop. And the diary / journal form allows for a continuous sequence of setup and surprise because of the way we often use journals to think ahead to new events and then reflect back on them when they are done. For example, the following entries set up a humorous pattern of inflated expectation followed by deflated reality.

> The Football Journal
> Day 1
> Dad says the first day of practice will be great. I am going to dazzle the coach with my speed, my strong arm, and my knowledge of the game. Quarterback, here I come.
> Dad lied. Can't walk. Too sore. Coach made us run so many laps around the track that we wore a canyon into it. Some of my teammates are probably still trapped down there.
>
> Day 2
> I told coach that I was going to be great in the backfield.
> Coach said, "Yes, the back field behind the stadium would be a fine place for you."

Notice that these work almost like jokes.

➢ Think of an ongoing sequence of events that could be chronicled over time—a sports season, a year in band, a New Year's resolution diet in January, the first two weeks at a new job. Then brainstorm a list of what's funny about that sequence of events, and try to place that sequence in chronological order. Then write a series of short, humorous observations. These can follow the expectation/reality pattern of the example, though other approaches are possible.

For more ideas on humorous nonfiction forms, see the section on nonfiction parody in Chapter 4.

3

Light Verse

Humor is also a way of saying something serious.

—*T. S. Eliot*

Poetic Elements: A Comic Review

Perhaps no topic, except grammar, elicits such a broad negative response from students as that of poetry. Whether reading it or writing it, the majority of students find poetry intimidating and irrelevant, as does the general public (except perhaps those with a penchant for the bad verse found in greeting cards). This is a relatively recent development. Well into the twentieth century, poetry was published in most major magazines and in many newspapers, and constituted over 50 percent of the literature taught in public schools. Now only a handful of national magazines publish poetry and few if any newspapers, and poetry accounts for only 3 percent of the literature taught. There are several reasons that poetry has fallen from being the primary attraction of literary arts. And there is a reason that far more people are familiar with T. S. Eliot's cat poems (through their use in the musical *Cats*) than they are with "The Wasteland."

One might argue that the purpose behind the origins of poetry was twofold: to remember and to entertain. Poetry likely predates literacy and served as a mnemonic device in recalling long stories and histories. The rhyme and rhythm made the memorization of such long texts easier. In addition, the rhyme and rhythm made listening to these stories and histories more pleasing—a kind of soundtrack to accompany the images created by the poems. Later in ancient Greece, shorter lyric poetry was directly linked to music (often accompanied by the lyre; thus the term *lyric*) and the "pop song" was born. The popularity of choruses singing such songs led, in turn, to the use of poetry in writing plays. In nearly all these cases and for the next 2,500 years, the intended audience was a general educated public. And the language of the poems reflected that audience.

However, this focus on story, song, the music of rhyme and rhythm, and—most important—a sense of the general educated populace as audience fell out of favor in the twentieth century. To grossly oversimplify, following on the development of free verse in the nineteenth century, which began to undermine the use of rhyme and rhythm, high modernists such as Eliot began to dramatically alter perceptions of audience, crafting poetry that was no longer meant for a general educated populace, but an audience of literary elite. The erudite language, the heavy use of allusions, the modernist fragmentation, all made such poetry virtually impenetrable by the average reader. In effect, high modernist poets wrote for other high modernist poets and for critics, professors, and teachers who found that the difficulty of these texts placed them in the position of priest-like interpreters of the word. Despite the fact that these are amazingly thoughtful, beautifully crafted poems that offer an important resistance to the core of American anti-intellectualism, the end result has been a separation of poetry from the people.

To be sure, there were and continue to be strands of poetry that attempt to appeal to the general population of educated readers, from William Carlos Williams's low modernist poems about red wheelbarrows, plums, and the poor, to contemporary spoken word and slam poets. And, perhaps more significant, the emergence of pop music has largely replaced the role that lyric poetry once played in the popular mind. There are many advocates for using such poetry as a means toward easing students into the genre. None of this, however, changes the fact that most students don't trust and don't like poetry.

One possible approach to making poetry more appealing takes a path directly through humor. It is no accident (though perhaps cosmically ironic) that Macavity the Mystery Cat is more widely known than Prufrock. Does this mean that I'm suggesting abandoning the poetic canon? No. Rather, as with the other suggestions in this book, I believe that we can let humor do some of the difficult work that might set the stage for the study of more serious poetry or serve as a kind of comic relief from the seriousness of most of the canon. For this we will turn to an exploration of light verse.

Light Verse

The term *light verse* generally refers to humorous poetry that can come in many forms—from couplets to limericks to long, mock epics—and with many intentions

—from the gently playful to the bitingly satirical. More often than not, light verse relies on formal structures, ample wordplay, puns, much alliteration, incongruous figurative language, and a heavy, creative use of rhyme (though there are, of course, exceptions to all of these). Though the term *light verse* suggests that these poems focus on trivial topics, that is often not the case. The humor of much light verse is directed toward moral misdeeds, political chicanery, and the social silliness that would pass for common sense. For example, when Alma Denny writes,

> What shall a woman
> Do with her ego
> Faced with the choice
> That it go or he go? (28)

she is addressing a fundamental question about relations between men and women in a patriarchal culture. What could be the argument at the core of a serious essay on human behavior (or a self-help book such as Jordan Paul and Mary Paul's *Do I Have to Give Up Me to Be Loved by You?*) is instead a tool for a humorous critique. Which will have a greater impact—the logical challenge of the essay or the barb of a funny poem? Hard to say, but the important point here is that both may serve a common goal. In this sense, light verse may be light in its approach, but perhaps not in its intentions.

Which isn't to deny that much light verse is merely for the fun of the language. From our experiences as young readers with Dr. Seuss and Shel Silverstein, we know the pleasure of funny, musical language. The popularity among young people of Weird Al Yankovic, or the comic songwriting duo Flight of the Chonchords, or Monty Python songs can attest that this pleasure does not die out as we grow older.

In any case, because of its frequent attention to form and style, light verse can be used in teaching students a few of the technical aspects of poetry. And it has the advantage of being accessible to students. Although university professors might prefer inaccessible poetry because of the opportunities it provides for them to demonstrate their own critical genius, light verse generally allows secondary students to feel empowered as readers, and it makes the idea of writing poetry more appealing as well. If someone questions the value of light verse, try asking, "What do Horace and Catallus, Swift and Pope, Auden and Eliot, all have in common?" The answer, of course, is that they were all practitioners of light verse. And if they found value in it, why shouldn't we?

The Elements of Light Verse

In addition to the general humor strategies introduced in Chapters 1 and 2, such as exaggeration, misdirection, and the rule of three, the core of light verse rests in just a few poetic elements: alliteration, onomatopoeia, metaphor and simile, rhyme, and feet and meter. So we'll start with these before looking at a variety of light verse forms.

Alliteration

The repetition of the same or similar sounds at the beginning of words in a poem has a long tradition. Anglo-Saxon and Old English poetry was often in the form of what we call *alliterative verse,* using repetition of initial sounds (rather than end rhymes) as a primary formal device. Although such alliterative verse largely died out in the fifteenth century, poets including Ezra Pound, W. H. Auden, and J. R. R. Tolkien continued to experiment with it. However, in most serious poetry, alliteration is generally used in moderation, and too much sounds contrived and comical. Fortunately for our students, in light verse "contrived and comical" are valued traits that can contribute to the humor of a poem. As we work to help them understand the idea of writing in different genres for different audiences and a variety of purposes, this shift from serious to silly serves as a good guide.

There are a number of exercises students can tackle with alliteration. The simplest is the creation of an alliterative alphabet book that begins with a sentence with nearly all words beginning with the letter *A* (with the exception of articles, prepositions, and conjunctions) and works through to the twenty-sixth sentence using words beginning with *Z*. (See Graeme Base's *Animalia* for an example with amazing illustrations.) These have the tendency to take the form of tongue twisters.

> The terrible teacher tried to trick the terrific teen.

Because there is some diminishing return in having individual students write out all twenty-six lines, this might work best as a quick group project, with each student assigned several letters and the whole group taking on the challenge of letters *Q*, *X*, and *Z*. Extra points if they can work in a bit of exaggeration in each line.

➢ In small groups, choose an audience of either peers or first graders. Brainstorm topics appropriate to the audience. Perhaps choose sports, pop stars, or middle or high school culture for older students: "The lard-laden lunch left Larry lurching late to Latin." Try animals, superheroes, or school for younger students: "Cuddling carelessly, the colossal cat crushed cute Cathy." Divide the letters of the alphabet evenly among your group members, and then each of you write the several alliterative sentences for the letters assigned to you. (Of course, these beg for goofy illustrations as well.)

Bruce Lansky, in his lesson "How to Write a Newfangled Tongue Twister," suggests having students write alliterative stories based on original tongue twisters. The challenge here is to see if one can sustain the story for several sentences while keeping to the same initial sound.

1. Choose a common tongue twister and then think of a possible plot topic upon which the alliterative story might focus—for example, Peter Piper as a Private Eye.
2. Brainstorm a list of corresponding alliterative words that might contribute to that topic. (This is also an opportunity for a bit of dictionary work where students skim through the appropriate letter entries scanning for useful words. When writing these I have found verbs to be the most crucial in opening up plot possibilities, so you might want to suggest that they to look especially for those.)
3. Begin with the first couple of words of the original tongue twister to set the allusion and then begin to construct, line by line, a quick plot that works to a conclusion. For example, one might begin:
   Peter Piper packed a pistol—Peter Piper the Private Eye. Peter pursued pesky pirates for pinching pastries and plum pie. But the pie rats fooled poor Peter by placing peppers in the park. Peter's penchant for things pickled proved the pirates pretty smart.

If you would like to share with older students a more serious, extended prose experiment with alliteration, see the first chapter of Walter Abish's novel *Alphabetical Africa*, which begins,

> Ages ago, Alex, Allen and Alva arrived at Antibes, and Alva allowing all, allowing anyone, against Alex's admonition, against Allen's angry assertion: another African amusement . . . anyhow, as all argued, an awesome African army assembled

and arduously advanced against an African anthill, assiduously annihilating ant after ant, and afterward, Alex astonishingly accuses Albert as also accepting Africa's antipodal ant annexation. (1)

Onomatopoeia

The idea of words imitating sounds intrigues us, from Old MacDonald's "a quack quack here" to the punching sound effects—"biff, pow"—used in graphic novels and manga. Writers of light verse often embrace the *onomatopoeia* for both its descriptive potential and its occasional silliness. To begin with, we'll focus on using onomatopoeia to help develop brief description. This works best if students have a subject in mind.

➢ Start by brainstorming lists of onomatopoeic words according to subjects. For example:

People	Water	Sports	Music	Cooking
cough	splash	crunch	clang	sizzle
hack	splish	pop	twang	pop
wheeze	drip	tweet	trill	crackle
sspptt	sputter	squeak	ping	hiss
achoo	spatter	swish	ding-dong	bubble
shhh	spurt	crack	rat-a-tat	glug
oh	glug	ow	buzz	dribble

➢ Then create a simple, descriptive free verse poem describing that subject.

Here's an example of a poem a student might create:

Catomatopoeia

The old cat's claws
click
click
click
on the hardwood floor.
Tail swish-swishing,
it stops
at the door.
Then a howl

and a yowl
and one last meowl
before the tamed human
opens the door.

(See Eve Merriam's poem "Onomatopoeia" in *It Doesn't Always Have to Rhyme* for an example with water as the topic.)

Some students may be sufficiently intrigued by the descriptive abilities of onomatopoeia that they might attempt to craft entire poems out of them. For example:

Bird Hunting

Honk! Honk Bang!
Flip, flap, rattle, splash
Sploosh, swish swash
Nom-swash swish

Click clack, rustle
Flitter flutter Bang!
Flutter flitter Bang!
Rustle Rustle.
Dang!

Russell Goebel

Fun to write, these sound-coded poems also make for great exercises in close reading. "Bird Hunting" begins with a goose flying overhead; the hunter shooting; the struggling goose falling into the water; the retrieving dog jumping into the water, swimming to the goose, grabbing it with its mouth—"Nom"—and swimming back. The second verse begins with the dog running through brush to flush out birds; the birds fly up; and the hunter shoots, but misses both times.

➢ Craft your own free verse poem that describes a scene with nothing but sounds. Then exchange your poem with a partner. Write a brief summary of your partner's poem-story and then discuss.

Metaphor and Simile

A staple of serious poetry, *metaphors* and *similes* offer us a means to describe our world in unique ways that make interesting connections between two normally separate things. These two things are referred to as the *tenor* (the thing being described) and *vehicle* (the figurative object used for comparison). For example, in the statement, "My girl is a red rose," the girl (the tenor) is being described through the use of the rose (the vehicle) as a figurative comparison. The vehicle in the preceding example, however, is cliché and expected. To be funny, a metaphor or simile must use a vehicle that surprises the reader through exaggeration, incongruity, and the like.

By the time students reach middle school, they are quite good at using metaphors and similes in their own lives—"My brother is a pig" or "My sister eats like a bird." But these kinds of common metaphors and similes have largely lost whatever humor they had. So we need to show students how they might spice them up a bit.

First, we might look at enlivening dead metaphors by what I call *stretching*. Because exaggeration lends itself to insult and its parallel dangers, ask students, at least for this activity, to choose an object or event as a focus. Or, if they really want to write about a person, they should choose a famous fictional character or pop culture figure.

➢ First, brainstorm a list of common metaphors that might describe an object, event, or character.

That concert really *stunk*.

The spaghetti tasted like *paste*.

Point out to students how stale these are as comparisons. They are too familiar and bring no surprise.

➢ Next, "stretch" the metaphor, exaggerating the comparison further to renew its humorous effect. For example:

- That concert really stunk, like the smell rising from a bloated skunk rotting under the back porch.
- The spaghetti tasted like paste—like sucking on one of those glue sticks in elementary school.

Students might also apply a type of misdirection in the construction of silly similes and metaphors. As readers, we are adept at recognizing the beginning of figurative phrases, and we expect them to be completed in a logically creative way. But if the author twists the metaphor or simile in an unexpected way, we are left with a humorous incongruity.

> She had a deep, throaty, genuine laugh, like that sound a dog makes just before it throws up.
>
> The little boat gently drifted across the pond exactly the way a bowling ball wouldn't.
>
> The ballerina rose gracefully en Pointe and extended one slender leg behind her, like a dog at a fire hydrant.
>
> He was deeply in love. When she spoke, he thought he heard bells, as if she were a garbage truck backing up. ("Similes and Metaphors")

Each of these sentences sets up expectations for a serious figurative connection, only to finish with a bit of silliness.

➢ Create your own misdirection metaphors, and then shape them into free verse poems.

> She had a deep,
> throaty,
> genuine laugh,
> Like that sound
> A dog makes
> Just before
> It throws up.

Next, students might consider using *synecdoche*, that figure-of-speech cousin to metaphor in which a part of something is used to refer to the whole. For example, "all *hands* on deck" uses the sailors' hands as a means of referring to whole persons.

➢ Brainstorm a list of common synecdoche usage, and reflect on what the effect or purpose of each might be.

Have students continue with this activity:

➢ Make a list of descriptors, associations, or actions about the following human body parts.

feet	hands	hair	hips	lips
eyes	ears	nose	arms	legs

These descriptors should suggest one meaning when referring to the part, but another meaning when applied to the whole person. For example, we might make a list for hands that includes such things as these:

weathered	won't fit in gloves	soft
touches	claps	shakes a hand
bejeweled	makes a fist	

Notice that saying someone's hands are "soft" or "weathered" or "won't fit in gloves" means something quite different from using those same words to refer to the whole person.

Once students have had a chance to think about how parts might suggest meanings about the whole, share with them the following Lucille Clifton poem:

homage to my hips

these hips are big hips.
they need space to
move around in.
they don't fit into little
petty places. these hips
are free hips.
they don't like to be held back.
these hips have never been enslaved,
they go where they want to go
they do what they want to do.
these hips are mighty hips.
these hips are magic hips.
i have known them
to put a spell on a man and
spin him like a top! (168)

➢ Consider the following questions:

Is this a poem about "hips"?

How does our understanding of such descriptors as "big," "free," "mighty," and "magic" change because of our understanding of synecdoche?

➢ Create your own "boasting" poem using synecdoche about a single (appropriate) body part, using Clifton's poem as a model.

Clifton's use of hips verges on what we refer to as *personification*—the giving of human or animal qualities to inanimate objects or ideas. Many serious poets use this particular kind of metaphor and simile; for example, Eliot equates the movement of fog to that of cats in his poem "The Love Song of J. Alfred Prufrock." Carl Sandburg uses that same comparison in his poem "The Fog." This might serve as a useful jumping-off point for more humorous uses of such personification.

- ➢ Using either a metaphor or simile, describe a weather-related thing, using a surprising vehicle for humorous effect; for example, "The hurricane, like my father, lectured us in a rage about the importance of being prepared."
- ➢ Try creating humorous personifications for your television, computer, bicycle, bus, car, or school building.
- ➢ Listen to and discuss Frank Sinatra's version of the song "Luck be a Lady," and then create humorous personifications for such abstract concepts as love, hate, jealousy, respect, joy, sadness, victory, or defeat.

Finally, for a humorous look at the ways in which serious, if romantic, poets have abused metaphor and simile in the name of love, students can look at the Billy Collins poem "Litany." Inspired by a poem by Jacques Crickillon, whose over-the-top metaphorical descriptions of his love elicit unintended humor, the persona of Collins's poem goes on to list a series of amusing metaphors to describe a lover and beloved.

Litany

You are the bread and the knife,
the crystal goblet and the wine.
You are the dew on the morning grass
and the burning wheel of the sun.
You are the white apron of the baker,
and the marsh birds suddenly in flight.

However, you are not the wind in the orchard,
the plums on the counter,
or the house of cards.
And you are certainly not the pine-scented air.
There is no way you are the pine-scented air.

It is possible that you are the fish under the bridge,
maybe even the pigeon on the general's head,
but you are not even close
to being the field of cornflowers at dusk.

And a quick look in the mirror will show
that you are neither the boots in the corner
nor the boat asleep in its boathouse.

It might interest you to know,
speaking of the plentiful imagery of the world,
that I am the sound of rain on the roof.

I also happen to be the shooting star,
the evening paper blowing down an alley,
and the basket of chestnuts on the kitchen table.

I am also the moon in the trees
and the blind woman's teacup.
But don't worry, I am not the bread and the knife.
You are still the bread and the knife.
You will always be the bread and the knife,
not to mention the crystal goblet and—somehow—the wine. (69–70)

The poem, along with the epigraph by Crickillon, can be found online at www.poetryfoundation.org and Collins can be heard reading the poem in several YouTube videos.

Shakespeare does something similar in Sonnet 130, which begins, "My mistress' eyes are nothing like the sun." But both he and Collins are a bit reserved, and students can push the humor boundary even more, especially if they assume that the persona is a bit annoyed with his or her lover.

> ➢ Use the following template based on "Litany" and create a "rocky romance" or "breakup" poem. Avoid "personal poems." Rather, choose two celebrities or fictional characters (Katherine and Petruchio, Heathcliff and Catherine) who have broken up or have a tension-filled relationship, then brainstorm characteristics, events, symbols, and other associations that might be translated into metaphor. Finally, write the poem from one of those characters' point of view.

You are the ________________ and the ________________,
the ________________ and the ________________.
You are the ________________
and the ________________.
You are the ________________,
and the ________________.

However, you are not the ________________,
the ________________,
or the ________________.
And you are certainly not the ________________.
There is no way you are the ________________.

It is possible that you are the ________________,
maybe even the ________________,
but you are not even close
to being the ________________.

And a quick look in the mirror will show
that you are neither the ________________
nor the ________________.

It might interest you to know,
speaking of the plentiful imagery of the world,
that I am the ________________.

I also happen to be the ________________,
the ________________
and the ________________.

I am also the ________________
and the ________________.
But don't worry, I'm not ________________. (Repeat metaphors from lines 1 and 2 in this stanza.)
You are still the ________________.
You will always be the ________________,
not to mention the ________________ and—somehow—the ________________.

The following example incorporates movie titles as metaphors for the lost relationship of Nicole Kidman and Tom Cruise.

From Nicole to Tom

You are the chewed gum and the discarded wrapper,
the popsicle stick and the empty bag of chips.
You are the color of money
and the human stain.
You are the invasion,
and the war of the worlds.

However, you are not the legend,
the days of thunder,
or the player.
And you are certainly not the leading man.
There is just no way that you are the leading man.

It is possible that you are the risky business,
maybe even the mission impossible,
but you are not even close
to being the top gun.

And a quick look in the mirror will show
that you are neither the white knight
nor the charming prince.

It might interest you to know,
speaking of the plentiful imagery of the world,
that I am the warm Australian breeze.

I also happen to be the peacemaker,
the magnolia
and all the right moves.

I am also the cocktail
and the urban cowgirl.
But don't worry, I'm not the chewed gum.
You are still the chewed gum.
You will always be the chewed gum,
not to mention the popsicle stick and—somehow—the empty bag of chips.

Rhyme

Most humorous poetry relies heavily on rhyme, not only for the musical quality it provides, but often as the source of humor itself. Though students are generally familiar with full rhyme at the ends of lines, introducing them to other

TABLE 3.1: Types of Rhyme

Types	Features	Examples
Full Rhyme	The last syllable, though perhaps beginning with a different sound, ends exactly the same	cry — tie hat — combat
Double Rhyme	The sounds of the last two syllables of a line match	legal — eagle myself — mice elf
Triple Rhyme	The sounds of the last three syllables of a line match	fearfully — tearfully
Forced Rhyme	An almost matching set of sounds is created by misspelling a word, inviting a mispronunciation, or coining a portmanteau	rhinoceros — prepoceros intellectual — hen-pecked you all

types of rhyme can broaden their options, sometimes making rhyming easier and sometimes making it funnier. Share with them Table 3.1.

Because rhyme is the focus here, as we turn to writing we will temporarily ignore other poetic elements, such as rhythm and line length, and simply work on lines that rhyme. This is something Ogden Nash did frequently with great effect:

Everybody Tells Me Everything

I find it very difficult to enthuse
Over the current news.
Just when you think that at least the outlook is so black that it can grow no
 blacker, it worsens,
And that is why I do not like the news, because there never has been an era
 when so many things were going right for so many of the wrong persons.
 (383)

In his poem, Nash ignores most things poetical (rhythm, line length), largely relying on the double rhyme to give his observation a little humorous bite. This almost-free verse gives young writers a lot of flexibility and allows them to focus on the anecdote and the rhyme.

➢ Write a six-line poem that focuses on an observation or anecdote and that uses a full rhyme in the first two lines, a double rhyme in the next two lines, and a triple rhyme in the last two lines. For example:

Have you ever noticed that men and **boys**
Are completely obsessed with electronic **toys**
And whenever they browse in the aisles of **Best Buy**
They get that awestruck look as if they have just been **blessed by**
Mario, the patron saint of video gamers, who approves of their **affliction**
And sends them home with new games to feed their mad **addiction**.

As students do this, you might share with them the following advice on generating rhyme.

1. After writing your first line, brainstorm possible rhyming words with which to end the next line.
2. If you don't come up with a word, use a rhyming dictionary or enter the end word of your first line in an online rhyming dictionary and see if something turns up.
3. If it's a two-syllable word you are trying to double rhyme, don't forget to include two-word possible rhymes: courage—your age.
4. If after all this you can't find a good rhyme, consider changing the last word of the first line to make for an easier rhyme (adapted from Richard Armour, *Writing Light Verse and Prose Humor*).

Forced rhyme is slightly more difficult because it involves altering words in a way that leaves them recognizable, yet closer in sound to the word with which they rhyme. Here, too, Nash excelled. In commenting on babies, he writes, "A bit of talcum / Is always walcum"—forcing "welcome" to become "walcum." And he ends his poem "The Panther" with the lines, "Better yet, if called by a panther, / Don't anther"—forcing the reader into a lisping version of "answer."

Another alternative is to coin new words. This works well with portmanteaus to create a rhyme. For example, here are two rather uncharitable ones that emerged from the creative teens in my household:

In the morning my mother looks a fright, as pale and vacant as a corpse **can be**.
Or like the undead in search of human flesh, perhaps she is a **mombie**.

I pity the kids that grow up **communist**
If it's anything like living with my **mommunist**.

> ➢ Still ignoring other poetic elements, write two forced rhymes, starting with a line that ends with a normal word (two- or three-syllable ones are generally easier) followed by a line with an altered word for rhyming effect.

Feet and Meter

Let's face it. One of the most difficult things for students to grasp in relation to poetry is the idea of rhythmic patterns, or *meter*. *Scansion*, the reading of meter, is a challenging skill for students who struggle just to make sense of a Shakespeare sonnet, let alone recognize its rhythm. In fact, scansion is sufficiently difficult and sufficiently arbitrary that many poets and critics will disagree in their identification of a particular poem's meter. Although being able to identify the rhythm isn't always crucial in reading a poem, it certainly is a contributing element in successfully *writing* many fixed-form poems. Because most humorous verse depends on careful attention to meter, I don't want to ignore the basics—even if those basics aren't particularly funny until they take shape in a light verse form.

To begin, we take a brief excursion into music. Explain to students that formal poetry works much like popular music in that it usually follows a particular beat, so understanding how beat and rhythm work in music can be a good way to understand how they work in poetry. For our purposes, two music types will suffice. Waltzes are typically in 3/4 time with 3 beats per measure, and rock songs are usually in 4/4 time with 4 beats per measure. Play students a short segment of a waltz and then a brief part of a rock song. Patti Page's version of "Tennessee Waltz" and the Beatles' "Love Me Do" are good examples because both have clear, easy-to-recognize beats. Have students simply tap out the main beat with their hands for each song, and then try to recognize the beginning of each measure as they count off 3 or 4 beats. Ask them how 3/4 time differs from 4/4 time in the way it makes them feel and the way they might dance to it.

Listen to "Love Me Do" a second time, and ask students what they notice about the drum beat. It has a distinct pattern of soft—hard—soft—hard, alternating from snare drum to bass drum (with an occasional extra beat tossed in). Explain that although 4/4 time may have 4 beats per measure, drummers can use that same beat in a variety of different ways by using different types of drums—bass, snare, tom, cymbals—and differing degrees of loudness (called *dynamics* in music). But ask students to assume for just a moment that there is only a single drum, and the only two options, while staying on beat, are to hit it soft or hit it hard. Have them brainstorm the number of variations that can be made with those two options using a 4-beat measure.

soft—soft—soft—soft

soft—soft—soft—hard

soft—soft—hard—hard

soft—hard—soft—hard

and so on . . .

These choices, involving only a couple of variables, allow for great creativity in music.

Formal poetry works much like this, using single *syllables* as the beat and the idea of the *foot* (typically a group of two or three syllables) as the measure. And the variation that a drummer can give a beat on a single drum—either soft or hard—is equal to the accent we put on syllables in English—unstressed or stressed. Reminding students of the patterns that they brainstormed for the 4-beat measure, give them Table 3.2, a chart of the most common beat patterns in humorous poetry. Point out to them that the stressed syllables in the examples have been bolded, and explain to them that the different beat patterns, or feet, are given specific names, such as *iamb*, *trochee*, *anapest*, and *dactyl*.

It's worth explaining to students that stresses are occasionally subjective; the way we read a line may be determined by the overall pattern we have set up. For example, in Hamlet's line, "To be or not to be," the foot "to be" is iambic, and the word "be" is stressed. But in the line I gave in Table 3.2, "Nobody likes to be," the overriding dactylic pattern that starts the line suggests that we read the

TABLE 3.2: Common Beat Patterns in Humorous Poetry

Syllables	Accent Pattern	Type of Foot	Example
2	unstressed — stressed	Iamb Iambic	When **stu**dents **tend** to **smile** a **lot** The **tea**cher **tends** to **smell** a **plot**
2	stressed — unstressed	Trochee Trochaic	**Those** are **fun**ny **lit**tle **ber**ries **Black** and **green** and **very hair**y
3	unstressed — unstressed — stressed	Anapest Anapestic	There was **once** a young **man** Who ate **noth**ing but **bran**
3	stressed — unstressed — unstressed	Dactyl Dactylic	**No**body **likes** to be **Close** to the **likes** of me

word "be" without stress. This gives students some flexibility, especially with many single-syllable words. For our purposes in generating humorous poetry, perfection is not the goal, but just a dominant rhythm to guide the writing. If students would like a mnemonic device to help them remember the types, give them the following popular verse:

> The **i**amb **saun**ters **through** my **book**
> **Tro**chees **rush** and **tum**ble
> While the **an**apest **runs** like a **hur**rying **brook**
> **Dac**tyls are **state**ly and **class**ical

Next, to emphasize the musical aspect of these patterns, practice drumming, using the soft flesh of the palm for unstressed syllables and the knuckles for stressed. You'll need to lead the students to keep time, and just work through the various foot patterns. Then, when you think they have it, you can give them an "open-note" quiz, drumming out a pattern and asking them to write down the type of foot. For a quick assessment before moving on, ask students to

➢ Write a single line of six syllables for each of the four patterns.

The last bit of technical information is how we describe line length in a poem, which is simple enough. Explain that when we refer to meter, we mean a combination of two things—the type of foot and the number of feet per line. In describing feet per line, the following chart will help.

Monometer = one foot

Dimeter = two feet

Trimeter = three feet

Tetrameter = four feet

Pentameter = five feet

Hexameter = six feet

Heptameter = seven feet

We combine this length with the type of foot when describing the meter or rhythm of a line; thus we would label the following lines this way:

Iambic Dimeter	When **I** ∣ de**scend**	Thomas Hardy, "The Robin"
Iambic Trimeter:	When **I** ∣ was **one**-∣ and-**twen**ty	A. E. Housman, "When I Was One and Twenty"
Iambic Tetrameter:	Had **we** ∣ but **world** ∣ e**nough** ∣ and **time**	Andrew Marvell, "To His Coy Mistress"
Iambic Pentameter:	If **mu-** ∣ sic **be** ∣ the **food** ∣ of **love** ∣ play **on**	Shakespeare, *Twelfth Night*

Finally, students also need to know that many poems use lines that either begin or end with a partial foot, typically an unpartnered stressed syllable. For example, William Blake begins his poem "The Tyger,"

Tyger! **Ty**ger! **burn**ing **bright**
In the **for**ests **of** the **night**

Here we have seven-syllable lines that begin and end with a stressed syllable. As we read the poem, we either fall into an iambic soft—hard or trochaic hard—soft pattern. It doesn't really matter which, and the poem can be scanned either way. But if we see the poem as iambic, then the first syllable *Ty-* is an iamb missing its first unstressed syllable. If we see the poem as trochaic, then the last foot is a trochee missing its second unstressed syllable. Again, the important thing to remember is that we want to create a dominant, consistent rhythm, regardless of whether we call it an iamb or a trochee. (See Joseph Powell and Mark Halperin's *Accent on Meter* for a detailed explanation of meter and a step-by-step introduction to scansion.) With these basic concepts introduced, students are ready to explore some simple light verse forms.

A Note about Topics for Poems

As students begin the process of writing funny poems, one of the first questions they will likely ask is, "What do I write about?" If you have introduced them to some of the basic humor and joke strategies in Chapter 1—rule of three, misdirection, pun, daffynitions—you can suggest that they try translating these into poetic form. In addition, you can have them brainstorm some of the topics shown in Figure 3.1 as possibilities:

As they begin exploring different forms of poetry, they will discover that different kinds of topics tend to work better with certain forms.

• Things you like • Things you dislike • Things that make you angry • Things you think are silly	• A witty observation • A funny anecdote • A problem with an odd solution • A question with an unusual answer

FIGURE 3.1: These are possible topics for humorous poems.

Forms for Light Verse

Couplets

Two-line rhyming *couplets* can serve as single poems and as building-block stanzas for much longer poems. As individual poems, they are similar to haiku, offering just enough time for a quick observation. When we expect them to produce a humorous effect, they often work like jokes, with the first line setting up an expectation that is then disrupted or distorted by the second line. The easiest way to get students used to this pattern, and a strategy used by many writers of light verse, is to start with the first "straight" line from a canonical poem—the more recognizable the poem, the better. It's generally a good idea to share the original poem with students first. Then show them how to use the first line to set up the misdirection, and then how to twist the poem with a second-line surprise. Here are two examples:

Tyger! Tyger! Burning bright, Thank you for the reading light.	(Blake, "The Tyger")
She walks in beauty, like the night Beware her vicious vampire bite	(Lord Byron, "She Walks in Beauty")

➢ Using the list of opening lines below or choosing some of your own favorites, create humorous second lines for each, staying as true as possible to the meter of the first line and ending with a matching rhyme (full, double, triple or forced rhymes are fine).

"Shall I compare thee to a summer's day?"	(Shakespeare, Sonnet 18)
"When my love swears that she is made of truth"	(Shakespeare, Sonnet 138)
"To be or not to be, that is the question."	(Shakespeare, *Hamlet*)
"There is a garden in her face"	(Thomas Campion, "There is a Garden in her Face")
"Water, water, everywhere"	(Samuel Taylor Coleridge, "The Rime of the Ancient Mariner")

"Full fathom five thy father lies"	(Shakespeare, *The Tempest*)
"Had we but world enough, and time,"	(Marvell, "To his Coy Mistress")
"Because I could not stop for Death,"	(Emily Dickinson, "Because I Could Not Stop for Death")
"Whose woods these are I think I know."	(Robert Frost, "Stopping by Woods on a Snowy Evening")
"I wandered lonely as a cloud"	(William Wordsworth, "I Wandered Lonely as a Cloud")

After students have a good grasp of how this misdirection works, they can try writing their own misdirecting setup line. This tends to work best when using overly romantic or slightly exaggerated claims about a person or thing.

➢ Create a straight line that follows a clear meter and that sets a clear mood, expectation, or claim. Clichés are fine in this first line. Underline the stressed syllables. Then write a twisted response line that follows the same meter and completes an end rhyme.

For a slightly more challenging couplet, students can try their hands at a poetic epigram—a two-line poem that offers a witty observation or states a truth and that often has a surprise in the second line. Here are two famous examples:

Little strokes
Fell great oaks.

Benjamin Franklin

News Item
Men seldom make passes
At girls who wear glasses.

Dorothy Parker

➢ Brainstorm a few observances or "little" truths that have to do with everyday life. For example, cats always want to be on the other side of the door, the note recipient gets caught by the teacher more often than does the note writer, iPod playlists reveal one's personality, and alarm clocks are evil. Then, consistently using any meter you like, craft a couplet that captures that truth.

Quatrains

Along with couplets, *quatrains* (four-line poems or stanzas) tend to be a favorite of humorous verse writers. In his book *Writing Light Verse and Prose Humor,* Armour suggests that

> couplets and quatrains are adequate for almost every occasion[. . . .] They are useable in the short poem or the long one. They are simple, easy to handle, relatively unrestrictive of the idea. They can be given additional interest and variety by internal and polysyllabic rhymes. (52–53)

These are the most common forms of quatrains in light verse:

> Iambic meter with alternating lines of four and three feet, with a rhyme scheme of *abab*
>
> Iambic meter with even lines of four feet, with a rhyme scheme of *abab*

So these might be a good place to start. Share the examples in Figure 3.2 with the students, reminding them about feet, meter, and rhyme scheme.

- ➢ Write a poem that follows an *abab* rhyme scheme using iambs of alternating four- and three-foot lines.
- ➢ Write a poem that follows an *abab* rhyme scheme using iambs in even, four-foot lines.

For each, use humorous observations, metaphors, onomatopoeia, exaggeration, alliteration, or other strategies for effect.

Although these can serve as a starting point, other meters, other lengths, and an *aabb* or *abcb* rhyme scheme can certainly work well (though an *abba* rhyme scheme doesn't project the musical humor as well as the other patterns

Alternating four- and three-foot lines, *abab*	Even line of four feet, *abab*
My **lap**top **runs** most **any** **game** From **Sims** to **Ha**lo **3** My **par**ents **say** that **it's** a **shame** My **lap**top **just** runs **me**.	When**ev**er **I** ar**rive** in **class**, The **stu**dents **turn** to **me** and **stare**. It's **rude**, I **think**, to **mock** a **lass** Who **wears** small **ro**dents **in** her **hair**.

FIGURE 3.2: These are examples of *abab* rhyme scheme.

because the *a–a* rhymes are so far apart). Students might try their hands at a ballad meter, which is made with quatrains of alternating lines of iambic tetrameter and iambic trimeter but rhyming only the second and fourth lines. Have them read and sing the theme song from *Gilligan's Island* to get a sense of the musical qualities of this form and how it allows for the telling of a story. (If you are in a particularly goofy mood, you can also turn some Dickinson poems into oddly comic moments by singing them to the tune of the *Gilligan's Island* theme song: "Because I could not stop for Death, / He kindly stopped for me; / The carriage held but just ourselves / And Immortality.")

After introducing these quatrain rhyme schemes, provide students with a variety of light verse poetry books, and ask them to look for alternative approaches to bring back and share. In particular, have them keep an eye out for how longer poems often consist of quatrain or couplet patterns (in stanza form or continuous text). For example, Armour suggests using a combination of quatrain and couplet, using the first four lines to set up the joke, and the last two to deliver the punch line. He offers the following example:

You Take the High Dive

Admiringly I leave the swan,
The jackknife, and the gainer
To the lifeguard and to amazon
While I do something plainer,

Such as by accident fall in
Or else, when no one's looking, crawl in. (*Writing Light Verse and Prose Humor* 63)

> ➢ Write a quatrain + couplet poem, using the quatrain to set up one expectation, and then using the couplet to disrupt it with a surprising exaggeration or reversal.

And, by combining sequences of couplets or quatrains, even without stanza breaks, students can create longer narrative poems if they wish. A long poem such as Robert Service's "The Cremation of Sam McGee" is technically in the form of octets, or eight-line stanzas:

There are strange things done in the midnight sun	a
By the men who moil for gold;	b
The Arctic trails have their secret tales	c

That would make your blood run cold;	b
The Northern Lights have seen queer sights,	d
But the queerest they ever did see	e
Was that night on the marge of Lake Lebarge	f
I cremated Sam McGee.	e

Yet it is simple enough for students to see that each of these octets is really just a combination of two quatrains with an *abcb defe* rhyme pattern. Such a pattern of four lines, with only the second and fourth lines rhyming, allows for a fairly easy extended exploration of a humorous story topic.

Clerihews

Extending the exploration of quatrains, clerihews are funny, four-line biographical poems written about specific people. Invented by Edmund Clerihew Bentley, these poems follow an *aabb* rhyme scheme, have lines of irregular length and irregular meter (though the last two lines are usually longer), and have first lines that name the target. Here is Bentley's best example:

Sir Christopher Wren
Went to dine with some men
He said, "If anyone calls,
Say I'm designing Saint Paul's."

The poem is biographical in that it refers to an actual historical figure, an architect who directed the rebuilding of more than fifty churches in London after the great fire of 1666. The poem is humorous in the specific context in which Wren is placed.

In general, it's best if students not write about fellow students, teachers, and others they know personally. Rather, their target should be a historical figure, a pop culture figure, or a literary one. To the degree that this requires they know something about the historical or literary figure, it becomes, at least superficially, an interpretive activity (see Figure 3.3).

Holden Caulfield Whined something awful He said, "You're a phony," To every Tom, Dick, and Tony	**Taylor Swift sings songs** About boys who've done her wrong You'd think the louts would begin to doubt Whether it's worth it to ask her out.

FIGURE 3.3: These are examples of clerihews.

You can find more examples, though not always classroom appropriate, in the honorable mentions of the *Atlantic's* clerihew contest at the *Atlantic* online (www.theatlantic.com/unbound/wordgame/wg825.htm#results).

➢ Select a historical or pop culture figure or a literary character, and brainstorm a few events or symbols associated with that target. Then craft an *aabb* quatrain, using the person's name in the first line. Don't worry about meter or line length (though the third and fourth lines are typically a bit longer than the first and second). In fact, the sloppiness of the form is part of its appeal.

Haiku

Probably no poetry form is taught more often than *haiku* because it is simple to explain and helps students work on concise, condensed language, concrete images, and careful word choice. Fortunately, these same writing skills can be practiced whether students follow the traditional content focus of nature, season, and reflection, or turn their aim toward the comic moments they see around them. You can insist that they abide by the traditional rules (three lines, 5–7–5 syllables) or allow them to give or take one syllable to make this a little easier. However, the primary goal is to first set up a moment, image, or scene, and then to offer a humorous twist. These may be silly, such as the following dog haiku:

> My human is home!
> I am so ecstatic I have
> Made a puddle. ("Dog Haiku")

Or haiku can be more subtle and wry, as those found in Siobhan Adcock's edited collection *Hipster Haiku*, which was the result of an online contest:

> Aspiring DJ
> Spins at Mervyn's on Sundays
> Mondays at Payless (11)

Or perhaps students might apply a playful Zen perspective on the human-computer interface:

> A file that big?
> It might be very useful.
> But now it is gone. ("Haiku DOS")

Most any classroom-appropriate topic is fair game, provided that it follows the form and includes a humorous surprise in the second half of the poem.

> ➢ Create a haiku that starts with a simple observation of an event or thing and that ends with a twist.

Tanka

The *tanka* is a Japanese form composed of a haiku followed by a couplet that has seven syllables per line. So it's a two-stanza poem that follows a syllable pattern of 5–7–5, 7–7. Like the haiku, the tanka has strict content rules in its traditional use, but for our purposes, the only restrictions besides the form that we will apply are as follows:

1. The first stanza (the haiku) must focus on a concrete image.
2. The second stanza (the couplet) offers a surprising twist.

These work much like the quatrain + couplet combination that Armour suggests. For example:

With her head so still and tail lashing side to side, the cat starts to pounce. With a thud, her nose leaves a smudge on the sliding glass door.	Elegant in black dress and pearls, the woman sneers at my Hogwarts tattoo. Should I tell her she's trailing toilet paper from her shoe?

> ➢ Create a few humorous tanka that begin with a haiku that captures a concrete image and end with an unrhyming couplet that offers a surprising twist to that image.

Psalms and Sermons

This category includes "poems" that vary a great deal in form and style. What they do have in common, however, is the potential for misdirection and incongruity. Psalms and sermons tend to assume an air of authority, a seriousness of purpose, and often a celebration of the sublime. As a result, the tone and style set up reader expectations in a way that is easy to disrupt. Simply by linking, for example, the term *sermon* or *psalm* in the title with a decidedly un-sublime topic, and then following it with a poem of backhanded praise, one can quickly generate enough incongruity to create that desired humorous tension (see Chapter 4 for more ideas on using forms for parodic effect). In addition, many psalms and sermons rely on parallelism for musical and rhetorical effect. For example, Psalm 27 begins, "The LORD is my light and my salvation; whom shall I fear? The LORD is the stronghold of my life; of whom shall I be afraid?" The pattern of repetition makes this form particularly easy to use for humorous purposes.

Greg Keeler, a poet and songwriter from Montana, is particularly fond of this strategy that uses the formats of sermons, psalms, odes, and even memos as sources of formal comic tension. For example, he begins his poem "Duct Tape Psalm" this way:

> Take our broken lives
> in thy bright grasp,
> and make them to hold
> fast until the bad weather.
> Make our down jackets
> to look like nuclear waste dumps.
> Hold plastic table cloths
> to the torn roofs of our
> convertibles and seal
> our cardboard windows.
> Make our hoses and pipes to
> spray sideways in many directions. (*American* 61)

In another poem, "Swiss Army Sermon," Keeler begins,

> Blessed is thy little saw,
> for it shall secure us
> blunt and tidy weenie sticks.
> Blessed is they combination bottle-opener
> screwdriver, for with it
> we shall pry many nails. (*Epiphany* 106)

The patterns that Keeler follows can work well for students. Name the thing and the type of poem in the title, and then repeat one of the appropriate introductory phrases throughout the poem just before describing, in exaggerated fashion, some comic failing aspect of the item. (Obviously, there is some risk here of religious insensitivity, though only in the adoption of form and common phrases, not in any real critique of belief. In fact, the examples that I share emphasize the way in which we have unfortunately replaced spirituality with materialism and an idolatry for technology. But a word of warning might be appropriate.)

Psalm	**Sermon**
Take . . . Make . . . Help me/us . . . Lead . . . Protect . . .	Blessed is/are . . . for . . . Rejoice for . . . (Note: use *thy* and *thou* as needed.)

➢ Brainstorm a list of everyday items that might be worthy of a psalm or sermon—an iPod, a computer, a pen, bubble gum, a bicycle, or a cell phone, for example.

➢ Choose one topic and make a list of the thing's qualities and/or parts and how these parts often fail us or work in ways that we don't anticipate.

For example, using the topic of cell phones, students might list these qualities and parts:

- *Vibrate* in our pants and cause us to jump in embarrassing ways
- Die when the *battery* gives up at the worst conversational moments
- Cause us to feel phantom *vibrations*
- Play an inappropriate *ringtone* in church, court, class
- Butt-dial (*keypad*) "What do you want?" "What do you mean? You called me."
- Create armies of *Bluetooth* zombies talking to themselves
- Distract drivers in intersections (*whole phone*)
- Provide under-the-school desk distractions (*screen* for texts, games)
- Texting and the ruination of language (*keypad and screen*)
- Cause thumb strain (*keypad*)
- Produce annoying one-sided conversations in restaurants (*whole phone*)
- A camera to catch our most embarrassing moments (*camera*)

➢ Next, choose the psalm or sermon form, and follow the corresponding rhetorical pattern while describing with exaggeration the humorous aspects you already listed. The more concrete the exaggerated images are, the funnier they tend to be.

Our list of cell phone failures might lead to the following psalm:

Cell Phone Sermon

Blessed is thy ringtone,
  for it will sing out in church causing grandma to swat the backs of our heads.
Blessed is thy key pad,
  for it can butt-dial our friends without our knowing. Hello? Hello?
Blessed is thy vibration,
  for it can cause us to jump and twitch in the middle of our class presentation.
Blessed is thy little camera,
  for with it strangers can take pictures of us passed out at the party.
Blessed are thy endless apps,
  for we know not what to do with our $5 anyway.
Blessed is thy Bluetooth,
  for with it we can all walk around as if we are hearing voices from God.
Blessed is thy text message,
  for with it we can sound as smart and romantic as Shakespeare – i <3 u :)
Blessed is thy battery,
  for it can give out as we try to call for help from dark alleys.
Rejoice and be glad of the conversations thou bring,
  for they entertain us as we drive mindless through stop signs.

To extend this exploration of the humor to be found in surprising combinations, you might ask students to brainstorm other kinds of incongruous pairings of forms and topics. For example, what humor can we generate simply by thinking of cheerleaders cheering for the debate team ("We've got logic, yes we do . . .")? Or what if they follow the star basketball player around and cheer when he or she eats breakfast, studies in the library, goes out on a date, or is pulled over for speeding? Such a sequence of poetic cheers could easily become a full-blown comedy skit.

Portmanteau Poems

For students who like their humor on the silly side, *portmanteau poems* offer a fun way to play with language and the opportunity to coin new words. As you may recall from Chapter 1, Carroll uses the term *portmanteau* to describe the mixing of the sound of two words to form a new word that contains the meanings of both original words. He makes ample use of such word combinations in his poem "Jabberwocky." In the first line of the poem, "'Twas brillig, and the slithy toves," he creates the word *slithy* from a combination of "slimy" and "lithe." He also creates new words in other ways, shortening words through odd word associations, but for our purposes, we'll stick to the word combinations.

Here's a fun example by Liz Brownlee:

Shoem*

Time Flizzes when I'm wrizzing—
Some words are toomely long,
And so I merge and jummix
To squeet them in my song.

It's really not too diffcky
To get my words to scrush—
Saves tromoil and timassle
When in a hurrid rush.

There's only one small difflem
For my puzzizzy head—
I'm baffplussed and conboozled
By what it is I said!

*Short Poem
Flizzes = flies and whizzes
Toomely = too and extremely
Squeet = squeeze and fit
Scrush = squash and crush
Timassle = time and hassle
Difflem = Difficulty and problem
Baffplussed = baffled and nonplussed
Wrizzing = busy and writing
Jummix = jumble and mix
Diffcky = difficult and tricky
Tromoil = trouble and turmoil
Hurrid = hurried and horrid
Puzzizzy = puzzled and dizzy
Conboozled = confused and bamboozled (300–301)

Notice that Brownlee keeps this a bit simpler with an *abcb* rhyme scheme that doesn't require many rhymes. This allows the focus to stay on the wordplay.

➢ Begin by choosing a topic, and then brainstorm words that are typically associated with that topic.

For example, writing about basketball, students might list these words:

basket	dribble	foul
score	crossover	pivot
shoot	travel	jump
shot	spin	pace
scream	man-to-man	miss
yell	zone	dunk

➢ Look for interesting, logical combinations of words that might be put together. For example, crossover + dribble = crossible, and shoot + score = shoore.

➢ Finally, work these words into a simple poem describing a moment or event related to the topic:

Coach *scrells* when I *missot*	screams + yells, miss + a + shot
Jacing about the floor	jumping + pacing
Until I *crossible*	crossover + dribble
Spround the defense and *shoore*	spin + around, shoot + score

Summary Poems

One easy way to incorporate a bit of humorous poetry into an already packed school year is to turn it into an interpretive activity in response to literature—perhaps just as an exit-slip activity, or as a more extended group response. *Summary poems* can take most any form, ranging from couplets to more developed poems, with the longer requiring more details from the original text and more skill with elements of light verse. The following example by Bill Greenwell offers a quick couplet summary:

Dover Beach

If God's the tide, He's on the turn.
So, baby, let our passions burn.

Students can tackle a slightly more developed interpretive poem, one that offers a judgment or commentary on the original text by presenting both summary and humorous critique:

The Princess and the Pea

The Princess slept uneasily
Upon a small, offending pea

And twenty mattresses that were
Between the vegetable and her.

Her royal person, rather plump,
Was agitated by a lump

That we, more hardy, would have said
Was never bothersome in bed.

Some people mind, and she was one,
The simple moral is, my son,

Avoid a princess, shun a palace,
And pick a wife more lean and callous. (40)

Helen Bevington

Depending on the time allowed and the depth of summary and critique you want, ask students to

➢ Create a couplet, haiku, or more extended poetry form to humorously summarize a reading assignment.

This can work well as a group activity because it tends to generate conversation about the central meaning of the text and how best to summarize it succinctly.

4

Parody

As Mr. Darcy walked off, Elizabeth felt her blood turn cold. She had never in her life been so insulted. The warrior code demanded that she defend her honour. Elizabeth reached down to her ankle, taking care not to draw attention. There, her hand met the dagger concealed beneath her dress. She meant to follow this proud Mr. Darcy outside and open his throat.

—PRIDE AND PREJUDICE AND ZOMBIES, *Jane Austen and Seth Grahame-Smith*

We live in an age of parody. From *Saturday Night Live* impersonations of political figures to *The Simpsons* remakes of *The Odyssey* and *Hamlet*; from Weird Al's comic songs to the more reverent parodies made through sampling and mashing; from the Bulwer-Lytton Fiction Contest for worst opening line of a novel—"It was a dark and stormy night"—to the Bad Hemingway prose contest; from fake histories to fake travel guides to fake apocalypse survival guides, we are surrounded by the repeating, remixing, and making fun of other texts. When Seth Grahame-Smith transforms Elizabeth into an expert in the "deadly arts" and inserts an invasion of the undead into *Pride and Prejudice*, we take pleasure in the friction between the nineteenth-century romance and the twentieth-century zombie/horror genres. Ours is a time that thrives on the ironic humor that comes from such juxtaposition of disparate texts.

These are guilty pleasures, especially in the classroom, because we are a little suspicious of texts that violate the requirement of "originality," and because such texts often make fun of texts we love. But parody has much to offer in terms of the skills we associate with English language arts instruction. It requires careful attention to form, language, and style, and insists that the readers and writers of parody recognize the constructed nature of all literary and visual texts. I would argue, too, that parody can serve as a valuable kind of critique, whether it targets popular films and novels or corporations and politicians. In this sense, parodic texts are an important part of the larger critical voice of a democratic society. And in some respects, this is an *authentic* type of writing for students, given that they tend to engage in it in their daily lives in small and occasionally large ways.

Parody Defined

Parody is a term about which there is much disagreement among critics and theorists. Etymologically, the idea emerged from the Greek *parodia,* which might be broken down into *para* meaning "beside" or "parallel to" and *oide* meaning "song." In this sense, parody is a text that parallels or imitates another. In its first uses, *parodia* referred to works that used the rhythms and language of epic poems, but focused on lighthearted, mock-heroic subjects. Such a poem paralleled and worked against the genre of the epic poem, rather than against any one particular text. There is some debate about whether the purpose of these early parodies was critical in the sense of ridicule, or whether they were merely meant for fun. Nevertheless, these early imitations set the stage for new kinds of writing.

There are two main contemporary uses of the term *parody*. The less common is found in the field of music. For a composer, parody is simply an act of reusing an established work or body of works. For example, when William Dix used the English folk song "Greensleeves" to serve as the music for his hymn "What Child Is This?" he engaged in parody of a serious kind. More recently, when jazz musician Jacqui Naylor smashes songs together, as when she sings the jazz standard "My Funny Valentine" while she and her band play a version of AC/DC's "Back in Black," and when DJ Danger Mouse combines the a cappella version of Jay-Z's *The Black Album* with a variety of samples from the Beatles' "White Album" in order to create *The Grey Album*, these musical artists create parodies that playfully draw the listener back and forth between the old and the new songs. (Check out "The Grey Video" on YouTube for a video version; some language is not appropriate for all classrooms.) Significantly, these recombinations are done for the purpose of making new use of the past and for the sheer pleasure of experimental creativity. They are not meant to be funny, though they often draw a smile when a listener recognizes them.

The more common use of the term *parody*, as it generally applies to literature (and film), is as a work that imitates one or more earlier texts for comic effect, usually at the expense of the earlier text(s). Fundamental to this imitation is a recognition and repetition of patterns of form, style, syntax, word choice, symbols, attitudes, and so on, that permeate the original text or a genre as a whole. But beyond this, an attempt to define parody in more specific terms becomes quite complex as it struggles to encompass a number of variables. For example, a parody may be a response to one specific text, a whole genre or subgenre, or a particular author or person's style. Although parody always relies in part on repetition of some aspect of an original text(s), this repetition varies in three fundamental ways:

1. A parody may imitate the form, style, or content.
2. A parody may be a full adaptation of the original, a condensation of it, or merely a parodic quotation of a part of the whole.
3. A parody may *ridicule* form, style, or content—or all three—or it might put some aspect of the original to a new use, revitalizing it in some way.

If we just multiply out the possible permutations in combining these three aspects of parody, we have forty-two different ways in which parodic text might be constructed; and that's assuming that these are either/or options, rather than the often overlapping continuums that they are. In addition, the humor strategies of incongruity, reversal, misdirection, puns and wordplay, non sequiturs, and slapstick are all typical of parody. But the application of these strategies varies greatly from parody to parody.

In addition, parody is complicated by the fact that it works like irony. Because irony refers to a statement that means something different from what it literally says, irony necessarily implies a complex and informed relationship between author/speaker and reader/listener. For example, if we hear the statement "That's great" uttered with an angry tone by someone who just backed his car over his bicycle, we are sufficiently informed by context and tone to understand that phrase as ironically meaning something equivalent to "That's terrible." If we are unaware of the context or tone, then the statement is no longer ironic, and we must take it at face value. In other words, irony only fully exists when a reader/listener recognizes it. For a student who has not been paying attention to the scenes leading up to Mark Antony's speech, Brutus may well be an "honorable man"; only careful reading will turn this phrase ironic. This is one of the central problems in teaching novels such as *The Adventures of Huckleberry Finn* or *The Catcher in the Rye* that rely so heavily on irony and sarcasm.

As with irony, parody requires a similar kind of relationship between author, text, and reader. Parody works as parody—it elicits the pleasure of "getting it"—only if the audience recognizes the connections between the parodic text and the original text to which it refers. In a recent *Get Fuzzy* comic strip, Bucky Katt wears a hooded sweatshirt partially covering his face, and responds to a challenge from his owner's father by saying, "I'm not the cat you're looking for . . . I can go about my business! Move along!" (Conley) Anyone who has not seen the original *Star Wars* (1977) will likely read this as merely an odd bluff, a ploy to escape. But *Star Wars* fans will immediately "get it" and take pleasure in the parodic quotation of Obi-Wan Kenobi as he uses a Jedi mind trick on the storm troopers who are searching for the droids, R2-D2 and C-3P0. In this sense, parody divides readers into insiders and outsiders; much parody is specifically designed to mislead outsiders toward a literal interpretation and reward insiders with a more complex one. Much ethnic, gender, and camp humor relies on these double meanings.

But what happens when there are no insiders to read the parody? If no one recognizes the reference to the original text, is the parody still a parody? This may seem like a trivial question, but at its root rests the question of how we define parody. Is it a type of text, a set of strategies, or is it a perception? If parody is something inherent to the text itself, shouldn't we always be able to see it? If it is an interpretive act on the part of the reader, can a reader "create" parody where an author did not intend it? Is it possible anymore to listen to an adulterous politician giving a lame statement of contrition, or a professional athlete talk about giving 110 percent without hearing a parodic repetition of the genres? Is there such a thing as unintentional parody?

Combine this confusion between author, text, and reception with the variety of types, purposes, and humor elements of literary parody and with the more experimental aspects of music parody, and we have a concept with enough permutations to make any inclusive definition nearly impossible. That fact can serve as a center for teaching about parody, as we allow students to explore a variety of texts that might continually expand the possibilities of parody as a literary form and an opportunity for creative writing. Students might begin with the following questions:

1. What is parody? What differences do you see among various parodies?
2. Brainstorm a list of parodies with which you are familiar. What seems to be the purpose of these parodies? What makes them funny?
3. Are there such things as unintentional parodies? Under what circumstances do you see such unintended parodies emerge?

Regardless of problems in definition, for students to become adept readers and writers of parody, they will need to be able to

- recognize a text, author, or genre's distinctive form and style;
- summarize a text and identify important or repeating ideas, images, and symbols;
- recognize that same form, style, content in another text or context;
- recognize incongruity, reversal, misdirection, punning and wordplay, non sequitur, exaggeration, and slapstick as sources of humor;
- analyze the parodic intentions of the second author;
- assess how the second text makes us reconsider the first text;
- imitate in writing the form, style, or content of a text, genre, or author; and
- apply the strategies of incongruity, reversal, misdirection, punning and wordplay, non sequitur, exaggeration, and gross-out and slapstick.

Notice that many of these encompass the core reading and writing skills that English teachers generally hope to pass on to their students. Though the humor strategies are, perhaps, the least central, they offer a rare opportunity for the kinds of divergent, creative thinking for which we praise most professional writers. Taken as a whole, there is nothing easy, inappropriate, or frivolous about these skills, and a teacher interested in making parody a subject of study shouldn't feel guilty or hesitant about such a project.

Parody of Poetry

We might begin a study of parody by putting some of those early definitions to the test. Let's start with the simplest: *a parody is a literary work that imitates another for comic effect at the expense of the first author*. We can explore a quick example that almost fits. Poems are easiest, in part because of their brevity, and in part because they tend to be distinct in form and style in ways that most prose is not. So we'll begin with a William Carlos Williams poem.

This Is Just to Say

I have eaten
the plums

that were in
the icebox

and which
you were probably
saving
for breakfast

Forgive me
they were delicious
so sweet
and so cold (74)

➢ Read the poem a couple of times, and then describe the form, style, and language of the poem.

Observant students might point out

- how closely the language of the poem matches the way a person might speak;
- how simple the words are: twenty-six of thirty-three words are one syllable, and all the words are common;
- how the poem is divided into three stanzas; and
- how the title and first two stanzas form one sentence, while the final stanza forms a second sentence.

In terms of content, students might observe

- how closely this resembles a note someone might leave for someone else (which Williams claims it was);
- how it begins with a description of something the persona did wrong; and
- how it ends with a request for forgiveness and an excuse for the behavior.

By our simple definition then, students should expect a parody of this poem to do some combination of the following: imitate the form, style, or content, and ridicule the original (and, by extension, the poet). Let's look at one that was part of a Guy Noir episode on *A Prairie Home Companion* featuring Garrison Keillor and former poet laureate Billy Collins (yes, poet laureates write parodies too):

This is just to say

I have buried your cat
Which you left with me for the weekend
And which you were expecting to pick up on Monday.

Forgive me.
She was dead.
So stiff
and starting to smell funky. (Keillor)

The student's first task (after laughing or wincing, of course) is to answer a simple question:

➢ What repeats and what is different?

In this case, repetitions might include

- the title
- the phrases "Which you" and "Forgive Me"
- the simple diction
- the content movement from behavior to apology to excuse

There are only two essential differences:

- The second text has only two stanzas.
- The second text focuses on different content.

With this in mind, students should consider the following list of questions:

At what point does this second text become a parody? (After the title? The first line? The last line?) Because the title is a word-for-word repetition, there is no parodic effect yet, no difference against which to measure the two texts. With the first line, however, a parodic effect is generated. If the parody ended with this line, we would still consider it a parody—though in the manner of a quotation rather than an adaptation of the whole.

Does it matter that the second text has only two stanzas? Does that diminish the effect of the parody? How much repetition is necessary to create the desired effect? The altering of the form from three stanzas to two does not seem to have much influence on the parodic effect. How much repetition is necessary is debatable, but enough is needed to keep reminding the reader of the connection, in order to sustain the humor. Parodies frequently condense or shorten the form or content.

> *What would happen to the parody if we replaced the title with "I Regret to Inform You"?* In this case, the title seems crucial to the parody. Replacing it with the more formal title strips much of the humor from the parody, even if we can still recognize it as a parody.
>
> *What is the source of humor in the parody?* As the previous question about the title suggests, the humor of this piece relies on the incongruity between the casual tone and content of the original poem, and the more serious nature of the content of the parody. Put another way, there is nothing "just" about informing someone that a pet has died.
>
> *What are the parodic intentions of the second author(s), and how does the parody change the way we look at the original?* To a degree, this is in the eye of the reader. One can certainly see an element of ridicule in the parody, a critique that asks us to recognize the limp simplicity of the original poem and its lack of seriousness and depth. On the other hand, one might see the parody as merely a playful reworking just for the fun of the humor.
>
> *What humor strategies are applied in this parody?* The first strategy is that of misdirection. The parody's use of the original title sets up our expectations, if not for a rereading of the original, then for something similarly light in topic and tone. The parody immediately undercuts this expectation by stating bluntly, "I have buried your cat." The second strategy is that of the gross-out with the use of "stiff" and "smell funky."

At this point, students might return to the original definition of parody: a literary work that imitates another for comic effect at the expense of the first author.

> *In what ways might even this fairly straightforward parody force a revision of that definition?* If nothing else, the verb *imitates* probably needs some qualification to something like "at least partially imitates." Students might also argue that a parody does not really need to critique the original, but just use it as a springboard toward humor. Of course students should be given their own shot at this poem.

> ➢ Create a parody of "This Is Just to Say." Be ready to explain the strategies you used and why you think your response qualifies as parody.

From here, a teacher could provide a series of parodies of poetry that further complicate this definition through examples of some of the variations of parody. Because our recognition of parody requires a knowledge of the original text, let's use a *Hamlet* soliloquy (below) as our original and explore a number of parodic responses to it.

Parodic Quotations

The simplest kind of parody of this soliloquy would be a short quote.

> ➢ Imagine a story in which one character is arguing the benefits of a vegan lifestyle, to which another character says, "To beef, or not to beef—that is the question."
>
> ➢ In what way does this statement function like a parody?

Anyone unfamiliar with *Hamlet* can only take this "To beef" statement at face value, a mildly witty acknowledgment of a dilemma. On the other hand, anyone familiar with *Hamlet* will recognize this as a parodic quotation, a bit of wordplay

To be, or not to be—that is the question:
Whether 'tis nobler in the mind to suffer
The slings and arrows of outrageous fortune
Or to take arms against a sea of troubles,
And by opposing end them. To die— to sleep—
No more; and by a sleep to say we end
The heartache, and the thousand natural shocks
That flesh is heir to. 'Tis a consummation
Devoutly to be wish'd. To die— to sleep.
To sleep—perchance to dream: ay, there's the rub!
For in that sleep of death what dreams may come
When we have shuffled off this mortal coil,
Must give us pause. There's the respect
That makes calamity of so long life.
For who would bear the whips and scorns of time,
Th' oppressor's wrong, the proud man's contumely,
The pangs of despis'd love, the law's delay,
The insolence of office, and the spurns
That patient merit of th' unworthy takes,
When he himself might his quietus make
With a bare bodkin? Who would these fardels bear,
To grunt and sweat under a weary life,
But that the dread of something after death—
The undiscover'd country, from whose bourn
No traveller returns—puzzles the will,
And makes us rather bear those ills we have
Than fly to others that we know not of?
Thus conscience does make cowards of us all,
And thus the native hue of resolution
Is sicklied o'er with the pale cast of thought,
And enterprises of great pith and moment
With this regard their currents turn awry
And lose the name of action.—Soft you now!
The fair Ophelia!—Nymph, in thy orisons
Be all my sins rememb'red.

William Shakespeare (*Hamlet*, Act Three, Scene One)

that indicates a flippancy about this nutritional/moral choice. As readers, we are amused (or annoyed) by this comparison and the way it evokes the far more serious indecisiveness of Hamlet. Students can also consider this question:

> *What aspects or elements of parody does this statement employ?* This parody relies almost entirely on style—the repetition of the same syntactical pattern of one line. Its only content concern is that of a general indecisiveness. In terms of humor strategies, it utilizes a simple sound-alike pun. And, when considering the question of attitude—ridicule or appreciation—in the parody's tone toward the original, we might err on the side of appreciation, a playful use of the original for a new purpose.

A similarly short parody based entirely on content, with no regard for the form and style of the original, might emerge in the same story if, instead of uttering the "To beef" comment, the character said instead, "I'm just an indecisive Dane." Such a parodic allusion generates the same comparison, though it lacks some of the humor of the first. Both of these examples suggest that extreme brevity is not a barrier to parody, and that any definition would need to acknowledge such a "quotation" as being at one end of a continuum. At this point, students might

- ➢ Brainstorm any parody examples of this "to be or not to be" phrase.
- ➢ Create several similar parodic quotations of "to be or not to be" and contexts in which they might be funny.

Parodic Condensation

Moving along that quotation—condensation—adaptation continuum, let's look at a slightly compressed version of the soliloquy.

Green Eggs and Hamlet

I ask to be or not to be.
That is the question I ask of me.
This sullied life, it makes me shudder.
My uncle's boffing dear sweet mother.
Would I, could I take me life?
Could I, should I end this strife?
Should I jump out of a plane?

Or throw myself before a train?
Should I from a cliff just leap?
Could I put myself to sleep?
Shoot myself or take some poison?
Maybe try self immolation?
To shudder off this mortal coil,
I could stab myself with a fencing foil.
Slash my wrists while in the bath?
Would it end my angst and wrath?
To sleep, to dream, now there's the rub.
I could drop a toaster in my tub.
Would all be glad if I were dead?
Could I perhaps kill them instead?
This line of thought takes consideration—
For I'm the king of procrastination.

After a couple of readings, the students should ponder these questions:

How does "Green Eggs and Hamlet" work as a parody? What strategies does it employ? In this instance, "Green Eggs and Hamlet" directly ridicules *Hamlet*'s content. In fact, while the first line grounds the poem within the context of the soliloquy, the rest of the poem condenses thematic aspects of the entire play.

Although the parody repeats key phrases and some issues raised in the play, it differs significantly in most other ways. First, one of the easiest ways to disrupt content in a parodic manner is to translate the text into an incongruous form and style. The title immediately announces this mismatch (with no misdirection), and we quickly see what happens to the soliloquy when done in the sing-song rhythm of Dr. Seuss. The playfulness of the rhyme, the repetition, and the rhythm all work against the seriousness of the question of suicide, as does the exaggerated list of ways Hamlet might kill himself. We might want to explore whether this is also a parody of Dr. Seuss, because the tension of the poem works in both directions; but more often than not, parody as critique works to bring down an elevated subject. As a result, we are asked to reconsider Hamlet in the original, to perceive him, through ridicule, as a rather goofy, creatively morbid, lazy adolescent boy. And, as we consider our extended definition of parody, "Green Eggs and Hamlet" suggests that room should be made for the ways authors condense original material.

Before moving on to another example, students might

- ➢ Summarize another play, novel, or movie using this Dr. Seuss style and form.

Parodic Adaptation

As we move across the continuum from a simple quote to a full adaptation, "Hamlet's Cat's Soliloquy" by Henry Beard will serve as a good example.

Hamlet's Cat's Soliloquy
from *Hamlet's Cat*
By William Shakespeare's Cat

To go outside, and there perchance to stay
Or to remain within: that is the question:
Whether 'tis better for a cat to suffer
The cuffs and buffets of inclement weather
That Nature rains on those who roam abroad,
Or take a nap upon a scrap of carpet,
And so by dozing melt the solid hours
That clog the clock's bright gears with sullen time
And stall the dinner bell. To sit, to stare
Outdoors, and by a stare to seem to state
A wish to venture forth without delay,
Then when the portal's opened up, to stand
As if transfixed by doubt. To prowl; to sleep;
To choose not knowing when we may once more
Our readmittance gain: aye, there's the hairball;
For if a paw were shaped to turn a knob,
Or work a lock or slip a window-catch,
And going out and coming in were made
As simple as the breaking of a bowl,
What cat would bear the household's petty plagues,
The cook's well practiced kicks, the butler's broom,
The infant's careless pokes, the tickled ears,
The trampled tail, and all the daily shocks
That fur is heir to, when, of his own will,
He might his exodus or entrance make
With a mere mitten? Who would spaniels fear,

Or strays trespassing from a neighbor's yard,
But that the dread of our unheeded cries
And scratches at a barricaded door
No claw can open up, dispels our nerve
An makes us rather bear our humans' faults
Than run away to unguessed miseries?
Thus caution doth make house cats of us all;
And thus the bristling hair of resolution
Is softened up with the pale brush of thought,
And since our choices hinge on weighty things,
We pause upon the threshold of decision. (8–9)

Here, too, after a couple of readings, and with the original soliloquy at hand for easy comparison, students should explore these questions:

> *How does "Hamlet's Cat's Soliloquy" work as a parody? What strategies does it employ?* Students may comment on how carefully the poem imitates syntax, rhythm, many phrases, and the fundamental logic of the original while replacing the content of the dilemma with a cat's indecision about whether to go outside or stay inside. Beard's is a complete adaptation, with a reverence for the form and style that suggests no hint of ridicule of Shakespeare, only a celebration of the fun to which the form and style can lend themselves.
>
> The humor of this parody is generated in part by the incongruity between the seriousness of the original, with its elevated form, style and diction, and the silliness of the topic of the parody. It is effective precisely because Beard so artfully blends exact words and phrases from the original with such cat-like observations as "aye, there's the hairball" and "thus caution doth make house cats of us all." Of course, part of the humor of the piece relies on our knowledge of the inscrutable behavior of cats, which has nothing to do with Shakespeare.

Let's return at this point to our definition and ask: In what ways does "Hamlet's Cat's Soliloquy" suggest a revision or expansion of our definition of parody? This parody does not really ask us to reconsider the meaning of the original, but rather to appreciate the creative reapplication of its form and style. As a result, our definition now must incorporate a careful and complete adaptation with a reverent attitude toward the original. Bringing a similar reverence, students can

- ➢ Brainstorm daily dilemmas—to pack a lunch or buy at school, to study or go to a movie, to wear that dress or the grungy jeans—and choose one that seems to offer the most examples to explore.
- ➢ Write a full adaptation of Hamlet's soliloquy using your dilemma.

(Note: see Chapter 3 for suggestions on helping students write in iambic meter.)

One last example might serve to illustrate the variety of uses to which parody is put and some of the permutations it might take in poetry. In Chapter 21 of *Adventures of Huckleberry Finn*, Twain includes a parody of the soliloquy as written by the King and Duke, a couple of con artists taking advantage of rural Midwesterners in the 1830s:

> To be, or not to be; that is the bare bodkin
> That makes calamity of so long life;
> For who would fardels bear, till Birnam Wood do come to Dunsinane,
> But that the fear of something after death
> Murders the innocent sleep,
> Great nature's second course,
> And makes us rather sling the arrows of outrageous fortune
> Than fly to others that we know not of.
> There's the respect must give us pause:
> Wake Duncan with thy knocking! I would thou couldst;
> For who would bear the whips and scorns of time,
> The oppressor's wrong, the proud man's contumely,
> The law's delay, and the quietus which his pangs might take,
> In the dead waste and middle of the night, when churchyards yawn
> In customary suits of solemn black,
> But that the undiscovered country from whose bourne no traveler returns,
> Breathes forth contagion on the world,
> And thus the native hue of resolution, like the poor cat i' the adage,
> Is sicklied o'er with care,
> And all the clouds that lowered o'er our housetops,
> With this regard their currents turn awry,
> And lose the name of action.
> 'Tis a consummation devoutly to be wished.
> But soft you, the fair Ophelia:
> Ope not thy ponderous and marble jaws,
> But get thee to a nunnery—go! (182)

After one or two readings, students are likely to be confused by this parody. Either before or right after their first reading, they should be cautioned that it doesn't really make sense. With that in mind, they can then respond one more time to these questions:

How does this work as a parody? What strategies does it employ? Only partially attentive to form, style, and content, this poem offers language and rhythms that sound Shakespearean, yet are nothing but a nonsense compilation of bits of *Hamlet* and of *Macbeth*, strewn together in such a way as to fool the uneducated. Given its context within the Twain novel, the intentions of the parody are open to a variety of interpretations. The poem illustrates, first, the King and Duke's limited knowledge of Shakespeare. They are able to recall bits of the original, but clearly never understood it given the incomprehensible mishmash they create.

We might also read this as a measure of the King and Duke's low opinion of the general population, who they believe will be fooled by this re-creation. Or is that Twain's low opinion of middle-class America? Is there a bit of ridicule, too, of Shakespeare himself, who, unlike Twain, did not write in the vernacular of the people and thus distanced himself from them? Or does Twain parodically intend the King and Duke to represent learned Americans, teachers and professors, who foolishly attempt to bring Shakespeare to a hopelessly ignorant public? Or all of the above? This complexity of meanings suggests just how powerful and effective parody can be in the hands of a gifted writer.

Given this example, how might our definition of parody now evolve? Among other things, Twain implicitly suggests that a parody can ridicule or critique something or someone largely unrelated to the original text.

As you can see by now, the possibilities and permutations of parody exceed our ability to easily define it. For our purposes, just recognizing the various approaches that authors take toward this peculiar art will need to suffice. If you are interested in exploring the writing of parodies with your students, there is certainly no end to the examples. Just do a Web search for your favorite famous poem along with term *parody*, and you're likely to get a few hits. You might have students try the following:

➢ Read the following poems with an eye for form, rhythm, and style:
- "Casey at the Bat" (Ernest Lawrence Thayer)

- "The Night Before Christmas" (Clement Clarke Moore)
- "I Am the Very Model of a Modern Major-General" (William S. Gilbert)
- "The Raven" (Edgar Allen Poe)

As a follow-up activity, ask students to

➢ Create a parody of one of the poems by changing the content and adding your own.

"The Night of Our Prom Dance"

"I Am the Very Model of the Modern Football Player"

Or

➢ Create a parody by using the form and style of one of these poems to humorously summarize a familiar play, novel, or movie.

And, finally, students can see how this literary approach to parody might be applied to pop music.

➢ Listen to Michael Jackson's song "Just Beat It," and then Weird Al's "Just Eat It" (the lyrics for both are available on the Internet). What strategies does Weird Al use to parody the original?

➢ Choose a pop song and write a similar parody, keeping the form and rhythm, but altering the content.

Parody of Fiction

Up to this point, we have focused on poetry. Fiction presents different challenges and opportunities. The patterned nature of poetic form and style makes it relatively easy to imitate in a recognizable way. This is not always the case with fiction. For a parody to work, it must be seen as a repetition of form, style, or content. When it comes to fiction, form tends to be defined by plot, and it tends to stretch in length beyond easy recognition of patterns. In fact, one of the challenges of teaching novels is to help young readers recognize and track such things as multiple plot lines and repeating images and symbols. And to see a whole plot as repeating other plots, a reader needs to be familiar with several novels of a single author or with the plots that typify a whole genre. As a result, fiction parodies are rather difficult for young writers. However, with a limited focus on author's style, character voice, characters out of context, and familiar short genres, students can successfully meet the challenge.

Author's Style

Looking first at parodies of style, the immediate challenge is that few writers have a style sufficiently recognizable for secondary student readers. As with reading poetry, the students need to carefully identify repeating patterns. In fiction, however, those patterns tend to emerge more slowly and are often difficult to catch on the first read. Nevertheless, some authors have styles that are sufficiently distinct to lend themselves to imitation. Perhaps the two most parodied fiction authors in American literature are Ernest Hemingway and William Faulkner, whose works have inspired multiple contests of Bad Hemingway or Bad Faulkner. Let's use Hemingway for our example.

Ideally, students would have read a sufficient amount of Hemingway to recognize not only his style, but also the images, symbols, and themes that run through some of his work (bullfighting, war, bars, heroic yet emasculated men, unfaithful women, and so on). After students have read a few of his short stories or one of his novels would be a good time to explore such a parody. On one level, we might think of style in terms of an author's preferences between simple words and longer words, and between simple sentences and complex ones. So a teacher might ask students to examine a passage from Hemingway and consider just those two things. Let's look at a scene from *The Sun Also Rises*:

> I went out to find the woman and ask her how much the room and board was. She put her hands under her apron and looked away from me.
>
> "Twelve pesetas."
>
> "Why, we only paid that in Pamplona."
>
> She did not say anything, just took off her glasses and wiped them on her apron.
>
> "That's too much," I said. "We didn't pay more than that at a big hotel."
>
> "We've put in a bathroom."
>
> "Haven't you got anything cheaper?"
>
> "Not in the summer. Now is the big season."
>
> We were the only people in the inn. Well, I thought, it's only a few days.
>
> "Is the wine included?"
>
> "Oh, yes."

> "Well," I said. "It's all right."
>
> I went back to Bill. He blew his breath at me to show how cold it was, and went on playing. I sat at one of the tables and looked at the pictures on the wall. (115–16)

A rudimentary style analysis of this passage reveals that the passage has

152 words

- 130 one-syllable words (85%)
- 18 two-syllable words (12%)
- 4 three-syllable words (3%)

20 sentences

- longest sentence of 17 words
- shortest sentence of 2 words
- average sentence length of 7.6 words

2 sentence types

- 15 simple sentences
- 5 complex sentences (including 3 of very brief dialogue or internal monologue)

The most common form of modifier is the prepositional phrase, including ones beginning with *under, away, in, on,* and *at.*

The most important thing for students to recognize from this analysis is the simplicity of word choice, the preponderance of simple sentences, and the brevity of sentence length. These observations might be a first step in a Hemingway parody. (Other Hemingway passages would likely reveal his proclivity for run-on sentences—slinging a series of short sentences together without punctuation—but we'll leave that aside for now.)

For the purposes of this parody activity, it would be easiest if students used the Hemingway passage as a template, following as closely as possible the form and syntax while inserting new content. Because this simple style isn't funny in itself, let's make it just a little humorous by placing it in an unusual context, say the Jack and Jill nursery rhyme: "Jack and Jill went up the hill / to fetch a pail of water. / Jack fell down and broke his crown, / and Jill came tumbling after." The question is, how would Hemingway characters handle this scene?

Jake and Jill, by E. Hemingway

I went out to find the girl to ask her how much to rent her pail. She put her hands under her apron and looked away.

"Two pesetas."

"Why, Jack Spratt got one for half that."

She did not say anything, just started up the hill with the pail.

"That's too much," I said. "I only need one bucket of water."

"Try carrying it in your hands."

"Haven't you got anything cheaper?"

"You want a cup? That's a lot of trips up that hill."

We were the only people on the trail. Well, I thought, I'll only do it this once.

"Well," I said." All right."

I drew the water from the well. She turned back down the trail.

"For two pesetas you should carry the pail," I said.

She punched me in the face. We fell. I hit my head, tried to hold on to my senses as a bell tolled in the distance, or was it a lion roaring on a beach . . .

We could work to make this funnier, adding a few of our humor strategies, but our purpose for the moment is to mimic the style in a simple retelling of the nursery rhyme. Students might try something similar:

- Create a Hemingway parody using the "plot" of a nursery rhyme or fable, say "The House That Jack Built," or "Simple Simon." Feel free to add plot details to the basic frame.
- Create a Hemingway parody of a scene from a favorite movie. How might Hemingway have written this scene in fiction?

(Note: see James Thurber's "A Visit from Saint Nicholas [in the Ernest Hemingway Manner]" for another example of this kind of parody.)

Some authors have a preference for particular turns of phrase. For example, although Raymond Chandler shared Hemingway's preference for simple sentences and simple words, he also liked to add detail upon detail in an extended, choppy sentence or a series of very short ones. For example:

I put the duster away folded with the dust in it, leaned back and just sat, not smoking, not even thinking. I was a blank man. I had no face, no meaning, no personality, hardly a name. I didn't want to eat. I didn't even want a drink. I was the page from yesterday's calendar crumpled at the bottom of the waste basket. (*The Little Sister* 393)

This patterned sentence structure allows students to explore the various ways that sentences can be modified by adding detail through using concrete verbs and nouns, present participles, absolutes, and the like. And as the last sentence in the previous example might suggest, Chandler was also quite fond of over-the-top metaphors and similes. Here are a few of my favorites from *Farewell, My Lovely*:

> "The voice got as cool as a cafeteria dinner." (286)
>
> "He looked about as inconspicuous as a tarantula on a slice of angel food." (202)
>
> "His smile was as stiff as a frozen fish." (347)

Such figurative language in the stories serves two functions. First, it signals to the reader that the narrator/gumshoe is an insider, someone who speaks the vivid language of the mean streets. Second, it provides moments of light humor in an otherwise dark text.

Along with the choppy, additive sentences and the figurative language, Chandler and other hard-boiled detective authors also use their own slang to give authenticity to their stories. You can pick up the meanings by reading and deciphering in context, or take a quick visit to the webpage *Twists, Slug and Roscoes: A Glossary of Hardboiled Slang*. A few samples will do for our purposes:

Big Sleep, The: Death
C: $100, **a pair of Cs** = $200
Chicago overcoat: Coffin
Chin music: Punch on the jaw
Dame: Woman
Dish: Pretty woman
Gat: Gun
Gum-shoe: Detective
Ice: Diamonds
Lead poisoning: To be shot
Mouthpiece: Lawyer
Put the screws on: Question, get tough with
Rod: Gun
Sawbuck: $10 bill
Shamus: (Private) detective
Sister: Woman
Take a powder: Leave
Throw lead: Shoot bullets
Trouble boys: Gangsters
Weak sister: A push-over

With these stylistic repetitions identified and a sense of the slangy tone of the tough-guy detective story, we might return to our Jack and Jill nursery rhyme, only this time the hill is just north of Hollywood, and there won't be any water, just a bit of ice.

I put the heater in my jacket pocket, flicked off the safety, just fingered the trigger, not taking my eyes off the dame. I was no weak sister, had no intention of being anyone's sap. She walked ahead of me up the hill, hair shining, dress shimmering, step-by-high-heeled-step. She was hot, hot as a California brush fire in a gust of Santa Ana wind, hot enough to make a sadistic drill sergeant cry.

She stopped at the well, turned around, stared right at me, not blinking. Her eyes had that little sparkle in the midst of deep black coal, like she was creating her own diamonds in the heat of her glare.

"So, Jill, I've got the Cs. Where's the case of ice?" I asked while letting the doll see the snub-nosed bulge in my pocket.

"Right here, gumshoe," she said, pointing down the well.

I stepped over, looked down, followed the curve of her arm to a wiggling finger, no ring. I was a sap, should've seen it coming, but the dame was quick. I put up one arm, tried to grab the pail, water and all, felt it smash my crown. As my world went black, I heard a voice say, "Jill, help me tumble the bum down the hill."

Here, too, it's enough of a challenge to generate humor solely through the incongruity of the style and the nursery rhyme plot. A second draft to incorporate other humor strategies could certainly follow. Have students give this a try:

- ➢ Write a Raymond Chandler parody using the plot of a favorite children's book, *The Little Engine That Could* or *Goodnight Moon*, for example. Feel free to add plot elements as necessary.
- ➢ Write a Raymond Chandler parody of a scene from a play or film, or one that summarizes a play or film.

Check out "Raymond Chandler's Hamlet" by Jonathan Post. It begins,

Something was rotten in Denmark, rank and gross, as rotten as a dame named Gertrude in bed with her husband's killer while the caterer recycled the funeral baked meats for the wedding reception, at which the bride did not wear white.

Hamlet was sharp for a prince, good with a knife, but not sharp enough to handle his old man kicking the bucket with an earfull of murder.

My name's Horatio, Hamlet's gumshoe buddy, trying to stay clean in a dirty castle. [...]

Character Voices

Although many authors don't have a distinctive style that carries over from story to story, they nevertheless may be adept at imbuing a single character with a distinct and effective personal voice. These voices (rather than the author's style as a whole) can also serve as a source for parody. Authors of young adult novels so frequently turn to first-person narration because it offers the opportunity to capture the distinctive ways in which adolescents think and speak, by incorporating habits of speech and ways of thinking. So the first order of business for readers preparing for this kind of parody is to once again look for patterns—length of sentences; general length of a single utterance (is the character taciturn or long-winded?); or whether the character uses favorite words or phrases repeatedly, returns to favorite topics of conversation, and continually exudes a particular attitude or tone. If we take Holden from *The Catcher in the Rye* and try to create a list of speech characteristics, students might notice these tendencies:

Begins sentences with relative clauses and phrases that draw attention to his telling the story.

- "If you really want to hear about it . . ."
- "If you really want the truth . . ."
- "The thing is . . ."
- "In my mind . . ."
- "No kidding . . ."

Uses brief sentences of commentary about the events.

- "I'm a terrific liar."
- "That killed me."

Uses "old" as a title of address for anyone older than school age or as a term of endearment, as in "old Phoebe."

Frequently uses "phony," especially in relation to social class pretentions.

Sprinkles the swear words "for Chrissake" and "goddam" throughout (you can, of course, leave these out).

Returns to certain topics, such as these:

- Where the ducks went
- Girls: "Girls. Jesus Christ. They can drive you crazy. They really can."
- Phonies and morons: "All morons hate it when you call them a moron."
- Kids, Catcher in the Rye, and the carousel

Armed with this list of tendencies, students could

- ➢ Write a parody using an exaggerated version of Holden's speech patterns to describe an experience that a hypothetical student might have in your school or community. (Remember to avoid personal references to specific people.)

To interject a bit more parodic humor into the project, I like to give the assignment an added twist by asking students to write in the form of a short reader's theater piece in which two characters, with distinctive voices but from different novels, meet. The idea is to choose two characters who are opposites in some way, whose voices are so different, and whose attitudes and views of the world are so conflicting that this meeting inherently becomes one of comic miscommunication. For example, what kind of conversation would ensue if Anne from *Anne of Green Gables* met Holden in Central Park? (It's unlikely that anyone would actually teach these two books in the same class year, but given the continuing popularity of both books, students who have read one book can pair with students who have read the other.)

First, we'll need to get a sense of how Anne talks. A list for her speech patterns might include these tendencies:

Uses interjections: "Oh, Marilla."

Occasionally breaks off into long, breathless descriptions of scenes and events.

Coins imaginative phrases to describe the world around her: "I shall call it . . . The Lake of Shining Waters."

Uses phrases such as "perfectly delightful," "splendid fun," and "so much more romantic."

Obsesses about such things as puffed sleeves, red hair, returning to the orphanage, and Gilbert.

A possible conversation might begin this way:

In Central Park on a bench by The Pond.

ANNE: Oh, have you ever seen such a glorious pond? Just calling it The Pond is so unimaginative. Don't you think it should be called "The Glistening Pool of Delight"?

HOLDEN: I don't know, maybe . . .

HOLDEN ASIDE: *For Chrissake, what a phony. She ought to get a load of what people throw into that pond. And what's with the puffed sleeves, that kills me.*

ANNE: Oh, I'm so sorry. I've forgotten to introduce myself. I'm Anne, Anne of Green Gables, and this is my first trip New York. And you are . . . ?

HOLDEN: Holden Caulfield . . . You got a cigarette?

HOLDEN ASIDE: *If you really want the truth, I guessed she must be a hick tourist the way she's all aflutter.*

ANNE: Of course I don't. What a nasty habit. You really should quit, you know. Do you suppose we could go for one of those carriage rides around the park? It would be ever so romantic . . .

➢ Brainstorm a few incongruous character pairs, choose one, and write a reader's theater script of their first encounter.

Characters

Most fiction parody tends to make use of allusions to well-known characters, character types, and genre elements. Students are familiar with these from such films as the *Airplane* spoof of *Airport* or the *Hardware Wars* version of *Star Wars*, or such genre parodies as *Scary Movie*. Though a lengthy adaptation of a longer story or film is generally beyond the means of most young writers, they can do something similar by either writing a short vignette of a familiar character or movie scene, or by parodying a typically short genre.

In writing a parodic vignette, students should remember the importance of repetition. In this case, the student will either (1) replicate the character and his or her familiar attitudes, speech, and actions, but place the character in the wrong context; or (2) replicate a familiar scene with new characters or "wrong" characters. For example, we might take the familiar character of Mr. Spock from the *Star Trek* series and make him the manager of a McDonald's restaurant. The more incongruous the shift in context, usually the better the parody opportunities. How would Mr. Spock's logic, his lack of humor, and his penchant for the literal work in the context of his largely adolescent employees and his impatient customers?

Always attuned to the readings of his scientific instruments, Mr. Spock recognized the bubbling hum of burning fries.

"Ms. Riley, by my calculations, you've overcooked the fries by 22.7 seconds."

"Like, just chill, manager dude."

"How, exactly, would lowering my body temperature improve your cooking abilities?"

This doesn't need to be developed into a full story (though it could be), but can simply serve as an opportunity for a short experiment in fiction parody and character study.

> ➢ Take a famous character from a play, novel, or film, and place him or her in an incongruous context. Write a short vignette or one-scene play using some of the humor strategies typical of parodies.

Conversely, students might take a famous scene from a story and replace the characters in an incongruous way. (*The Simpsons* does this on a regular basis by placing Homer and Marge into classic story scenes.) What if we replace Romeo and Juliet in the balcony scene with today's text-messaging teens?

Romeo and Juliet Text Messages
Act 1

LOGIN: Romeo : R u awake? Want 2 chat?

JULIET: O Rom. Where4 art thou?

ROMEO: Outside yr window.

JULIET: Stalker!

ROMEO: Had 2 come. feeling jiggy.

JULIET: B careful. My family h8 u.

ROMEO: Tell me about it. What about u?

JULIET: 'm up for marriage f u are. Is tht a bit fwd?

ROMEO: No. Yes. No. Oh, dsnt mat-r, 2moro @ 9?

JULIET: Luv U xxxx

ROMEO: CU then xxxx

(Roz Chast)

This should be a "natural" activity for most students:

> ➢ Translate a famous scene from a novel, play, or film into a texting conversation.

Or how about replacing the characters in a scene with a cat and a dog? (See Nina Laden's *Romeow and Drooliet* for one possible result.) For an extended version of this, check out the online *LOL Cat Bible Translation Project,* which rewrites the Old and New Testaments from the point of view of Ceiling Cat (God) and Basement Cat (Satan) using a distinct dialect and a set of symbols developed over time by the website contributors.

> Genesis
> Boreded Ceiling Cat makinkgz Urf n stuffs
>
> 1 Oh hai. In teh beginnin Ceiling Cat maded teh skiez An da Urfs, but he did not eated dem.
>
> 2 Da Urfs no had shapez An haded dark face, An Ceiling Cat rode invisible bike over teh waterz.
>
> 3 At start, no has lyte. An Ceiling Cat sayz, i can haz lite? An lite wuz.
>
> 4 An Ceiling Cat sawed teh lite, to seez stuffs, An splitted teh lite from dark but taht wuz ok cuz kittehs can see in teh dark An not tripz over nethin.
>
> 5 An Ceiling Cat sayed light Day An dark no Day. It were FURST!!!1

For a curious exercise in fantasy linguistics, check out the "How To Speak LOL Cat" page (http://www.lolcatbible.com/index.php?title=How_to_speak_lolcat).

Finally, students might use character and voice as a means of both parody and summary. Examples can be found in the book *Twitterature,* in which classic novels, plays, and poems are summarized in twenty tweets or fewer. Each tweet is 100 characters or less in the voice of the main character. For example, a tweet summary of *The Old Man and the Sea* begins this way:

> Forty days since I have caught a fish. And . . .
> The boy brings me the paper. We talk about baseball. I <3 DiMaggio.
> I am a strange old man. Perhaps I will grow a beard.
> I may have caught a big one.
> It is pulling hard. The coast is far away. May be home late.
> Still being pulled
> Still being pulled! (Aciman 36)

Genre

A number of authors have made a name for themselves with parodies of familiar stories from short genres. In *The True Story of the Three Little Pigs,* Jon Scieszka transforms the well-known folk tale by telling it through the wolf's perspective. James Finn Garner's *Politically Correct Bedtime Stories* alters well-known fairy tales by giving them a morality twist. What happens when Little Red Riding Hood is a feminist who finds more in common with the oppressed wolf than she does with the supposedly heroic woodchopper? Such short fiction serves as a reasonable genre for parody for young writers.

> ➢ Take the basic story line of a folk tale, but alter it in a humorous way by changing characters, character attitudes, setting, or some other aspect.

Using only fairy tale titles, Mike Richardson-Bryan suggests the parodic possibilities of crossing genres:

> *Klingon Fairy Tales*
>
> Goldilocks Dies with Honor at the Hands of the Three Bears
>
> Snow White and the Six Dwarves She Killed with Her Bare Hands and the Seventh Dwarf She Let Get Away as a Warning to Others
>
> (*McSweeney's Joke Book of Book Jokes* 53)

> ➢ Create a parody list of common fairy tale titles from the perspectives of vampires, cats, Batman, or some other incongruous point of view.

Students are quite familiar with the short narratives they experience on television, though they seldom reflect on this. Having them parody the typical plot structure of their favorite sitcom would help them recognize the formulaic nature of such narratives. For example, ensemble sitcoms like *Friends*, or even an animated one like *The Simpsons*, almost always have two story lines per episode: a main one and a minor one. Students might recognize the way each plot line within a sitcom tends to follow a two-act structure, beginning with the introduction of the problem in Act 1, followed by the worsening of the problem and then its resolution in Act 2 (see Chapter 3 for more details). One way to engage in such a parody would be to turn to meta-drama—a show about the making of a show:

> ➢ Create an episode of your favorite sitcom in which the characters recognize that they are characters in a sitcom, and that they are expected to act in certain ways, to have certain problems, and to follow a particular plot line. Give the characters the opportunity to argue with the author about the plot.

In the vein of *Pride and Prejudice and Zombies,* "The Edge" column in a recent issue of the *Oregonian* suggested "Taking the Class Out of Classics" by offering quick plot summaries of novels combined with self-help books. For example:

> *Wuthering Heights and the Women Who Love Them*
> Catherine realizes she and Heathcliff are sharing a love that is dysfunctional and co-dependent. She vows not to fall into shaming or blaming, but to live in the moment, enjoying their tender times together in the heather. But when Heathcliff gets morose out on the moors, Catherine tells him he needs therapy. He erupts into a rage and says she's the one with commitment issues. Catherine grows weary of the trauma drama and starts seeing Edgar. Desperate at the thought of losing Catherine, Heathcliff undergoes anger management counseling, and the two of them live happily ever after as heather farmers. (Peck)

➢ Write a plot summary that combines two novels, movies, or nonfiction texts that don't fit well together.

McSweeney's, in books and in the online literary journal, has quite a collection of similar kinds of plays with common stories and plots, including an editor's response to a rather inappropriate manuscript submission for a new Hardy Boys novel in Jay Dyckman's "RE: Hardy Boys Manuscript Submission":

> First and foremost, we are unpersuaded that the subject matter of The Case of the Secret Meth Lab is appropriate for our readers. We understand that the manufacturing of narcotics in otherwise bucolic towns has indeed become a problem. That said, we ask you whether Joe Hardy would realistically go undercover and turn into what his brother repeatedly refers to as "crankhead." [. . .] (Dyckman 23–25)

➢ Brainstorm an "inappropriate" plot outline (within the bounds of classroom expectations) for one of the many children's series books. Write a shocked editor's response to your plot.

(Note: see some of the *Pearls before Swine* comic strips for Rat's inappropriate children's stories.)

Parody of Nonfiction

One of the richest sources for classroom parody is nonfiction. In most instances, this type of parody is a humorous exploration of the form and content expectations of a particular kind of document. In general, the more familiar students are with the type of document, the more capable they'll be in recognizing its patterns and parodying them. To this end, we might ask students to identify the kinds of nonfiction texts they encounter on a regular basis—cereal boxes, shampoo bottle instructions, CD liner notes, cafeteria menus, TV guides, and the like.

Daily Items

We might start small, choosing something like the washing instructions on the little tag inside a shirt, or the side-effects warning on a bottle of medicine, or the ingredient's list on a can of energy drink (see Table 4.1).

Because these are readily recognizable "genres," a parody needs to simply repeat enough of the expected pattern to set up expectations, and then apply a strategy of exaggeration in order to make fun of the kinds of little texts we encounter every day.

> ➢ Choose a short "text" that you encounter on a regular basis in your home. Identify its common contents, language, and form, and then create a parody version using exaggeration and other humor strategies.

TABLE 4.1: Examples of Daily Items

Laundry Instructions	Medicine Side Effects	Energy Drink Ingredients
Do not machine-wash. Do not use bleach. Do not use hot water. Do not use warm water. Do not use any water. Do not even touch this garment unless you are wearing sterilized surgical gloves. Put this garment down immediately you clumsy oaf. (Barry, *Dave Barry's Complete Guide to Guys*, 188)	May cause marked drowsiness and dry mouth; excitability may occur, especially in children playing video games; may cause bad hair, green teeth, and an uncontrollable urge to do the hokey-pokey; continuous use may increase the risk of spontaneous combustion.	carbonated water, sucrose, caffeine, fructose, caffeine, citric acid, caffeine, taurine ginseng, amphetamines, energizer bunny extract, jet fuel, weapons-grade plutonium, and natural flavors.

Famous Documents

Because students are somewhat familiar with them, famous documents can serve as a great source for parodic humor. As usual, we want to retain and repeat at least one aspect of the original's form, style, or content. For example, we might retain the general content of the Gettysburg Address, but alter the form, as Peter Norvig did, into a PowerPoint presentation. Slides 2 and 3 of his presentation reduce much of the speech to the bullet points listed in Figure 4.1 below.

In this case, the humor is not directed at the original document but at the limitations of PowerPoint as a medium. In explaining his process, Norvig says,

> I wasn't a professional designer, so I thought I'd be in for a late night doing some serious research: in color science to find a truly garish color scheme; in typography to find the worst fonts; and in overall design to find a really bad layout. But fortunately for me, the labor-saving Autocontent Wizard took care of all this for me! It suggested a red-on-dark-color choice for the navigation buttons that makes them very hard to see; it chose a serif font for the date that is illegible in low-resolution web mode, [. . .] All I had to do was take Lincoln's words and break them into pieces, making sure that I captured the main phrases of the original, while losing all the flow, eloquence, and impact.

Despite the fact that the software did most of the bad work for Norvig, the project itself asks that the designer consider such things as color, arrangement, font, and language in order to recognize an exaggeratedly bad PowerPoint slide. And, of course, this example offers the opportunity to reflect on Lincoln's style, what makes it so effective, and why it's lost in translation to a different genre.

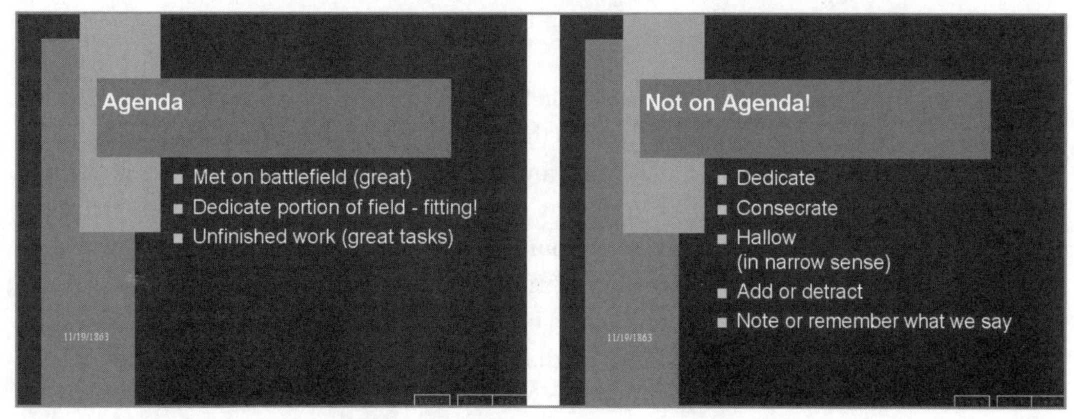

FIGURE 4.1: This PowerPoint stylistically desecrates the Gettysburg Address.

Engaging in a similar PowerPoint parody might also serve as a useful springboard into a discussion about how to improve student and teacher PowerPoint presentations.

> ➢ Create a humorous PowerPoint presentation of a famous speech, soliloquy, or historical document. Be sure to keep the core content the same, but allow the limitations of PowerPoint to "ruin" the grace of the original.

Alternatively, we might keep the general form and the content of the famous document the same, but change the style or voice of the original. How might Bill and Ted (from the film *Bill and Ted's Excellent Adventure*) have written the Bill of Rights? Or what if the character Cher, from the film *Clueless*, declares independence in a breathless valley-girl conversation with King George?

> George, I know old people can be so sweet, and we've been friends forever because we both know what it's like having other countries be jealous of each other, but it's time to split. I've only been hanging with you because there's, like, this major nation babe drought on this continent, but it's time to dissolve our bondage. I mean, your behavior lately has been, like, gross. Have you smelled the stink of the designer imposter perfume your soldiers wear? And those red coats, ewww. And this taxation thing, ugh, that's so five years ago. And besides, I'm totally crazy in love with Thomas J.

> ➢ Match a famous document with an incongruous character from a novel, film, or television show. Write out a piece of that document using the character's voice.

News

From the weekly *Saturday Night Live* skit to *The Daily Show* to *The Onion*, the news genre has frequently been the subject of hilarious parodies. The challenge for teachers here is the fact that few students are readers or watchers of print or television news. In fact, according to a 2004 poll taken by the Pew Research Center, upwards of 20 percent of young people actually use fake news sources like *The Daily Show* as their primary sources of information ("Young America's News Source"). I'd like to think this is because young people have learned a healthy distrust for a suspect news media, but I'll guess that it has more to do with a preference for irony and parody. Nevertheless, in order to parody news articles from a newspaper, students will need to have some knowledge of what typically constitutes news and the idea of "newsworthy," as well as how news articles are structured and the "objective" language of the news. So a study of newspapers may be prerequisite for any news parody activity. Once students understand the basics, they'll be ready to parody them.

➢ Brainstorm topics and headlines that make fun of the idea of "newsworthy" through incongruity, reversal, and exaggeration. For example, *The Onion* offers un-newsworthy articles ranging from international to local to business to sports news:[1]
  - Spain Vows Eternal Vigilance in War on Bulls
  - Elderly Man Skipping Work Uses "Dead Grandson" Excuse Again
  - KFC No Longer Permitted to Use Word "Eat" in Advertisements
  - Elf Finger Found in Box of Keebler Cookies
  - Kobe Bryant Proves He Can Win Championship with Luke Walton on Team

Students can now experiment with creating their own parodies:

➢ Once you have a headline, create a first sentence or two that summarizes the who, what, where, why, and when of the story, as in this example titled "KFC No Longer Permitted to Use Word 'Eat' in Advertisements":

> WASHINGTON—Issuing a condemnation of Kentucky Fried Chicken's recent Boneless Variety Bucket commercials, the Federal Communications Commission on Tuesday fined the fast food giant $600,000 and ordered it to discontinue all broadcasts containing "false and misleading suggestions" that its heated chicken products are intended for consumption.

➢ Complete the article with humorous examples and quotations.

Academic Texts

Students perceive most textbooks as dry and lifeless because, well, they are. But what makes them that way? Have students reflect on the form and style of their history textbook. Presumably they will recognize that it is characterized by several aspects: its overall chronological structure; its focus on important events and their causes; its focus on famous people; its attention to accuracy in terms of names, dates, and geographical places; and its objective voice. Each one of these aspects is subject to parody. How would a history textbook be shaped if it were written by a time traveler who experiences events out of order? What if we define important events in terms of romance? Or distinguish important people by breakthroughs in fashion? What if we continually give inaccurate information? What if we tell history in a biased, first-person voice? Any or all of these can serve as a starting point for a brief historical parody.

In *Dave Barry Slept Here*, the author explores most, if not all, of these possibilities. For example, Barry disrupts our anticipation regarding dates and places by first insisting that all important events actually happened on October 8, because that is his son's birthday and is easy to remember. He also gives us the same map for every place. He offers the following as a transition between colonial America and the new United States:

> Against all odds, the colonists had won the war against England; now they faced an even greater task: planning the victory party. Who should be invited? Where would they put their coats? These were just two of the questions confronting leaders of the fledgling nation. Also, extreme factions in several states felt that there should be some kind of government. (63)

In this passage, Barry undercuts our expectations of what is important, foregrounding the "celebration" and making the normal history a brief aside. Of course, in order to effectively parody an event, students should know something about it, so this activity has a sneaky tendency to make them study at least one passage of their history text with some attention.

➢ Choose a historical event and familiarize yourself with the facts. Examine how your history textbook presents the material. Write a parody version that distorts time, facts, and/or the importance of certain aspects of that event.

(Note: if students happen to notice how this activity resembles what some television news personalities do, so much the better.)

As long as we're on the topic of academic texts, we shouldn't leave out the kinds of documents that students receive in schools. Because they are already quite familiar with these, little preparation, or examples, will likely be necessary.

➢ Create a parody of a course syllabus that makes fun of either incongruous course content or exaggerated teacher attributes. (Be sure that you describe a hypothetical, exaggerated course and not a real one.)

For an example of funny course content, see Robert Lanham's syllabus description for a class titled "Writing for Nonreaders in the Postprint Era":

> As print takes its place alongside smoke signals, cuneiform, and hollering, there has emerged a new literary age, one in which writers no longer need to feel encumbered by the paper cuts, reading, and excessive use of words traditionally associated with the writing trade. Writing for Nonreaders in the Postprint Era focuses on the creation of short-form prose that is not intended to be reproduced on pulp fibers.
>
> Instant messaging. Twittering. Facebook updates. These 21st-century literary genres are defining a new "*Lost* Generation" of minimalists who would much rather watch *Lost* on their iPhones than toil over long-winded articles and short stories. Students will acquire the tools needed to make their tweets glimmer with a complete lack of forethought, their Facebook updates ring with self-importance, and their blog entries shimmer with literary pithiness. All without the restraints of writing in complete sentences. w00t! w00t! Throughout the course, a further paring down of the Hemingway/Stein school of minimalism will be emphasized, limiting the superfluous use of nouns, verbs, adverbs, adjectives, conjunctions, gerunds, and other literary pitfalls.

For a course based on teacher eccentricity, think of a teacher stereotype as the "author." In other words, what would a syllabus look like from an exaggeratedly hard-nosed, impossibly high-standards teacher? What would one look like from a bleeding-heart, hippie, rock-and-roll wannabe? How might these teachers' course descriptions, text choices, grading scales, class rules, and calendars differ?

➢ Create a parody exam for the course you have created.

How-to Articles

Anyone who browses popular magazines and newspapers (and the self-help section of the local bookstore) can't help but come across advice on how to do, make, or become something new. From housekeeping to dating to preparing for college to finding a job, someone somewhere has written a step-by-step explanation of how to do it. In constructing a parody of such texts, students will want to keep the form (a list, numbered procedure, or defined categories) because that is likely the most distinctive characteristic. To create the parody, they will need to either exaggerate the advice or focus on a topic about which such advice is inherently funny.

For an example of exaggerated advice, we might take the kind of holiday arts-and-crafts advice of Martha Stewart (some would argue that her advice is already a domestic parody) and exaggerate it just a bit. Students might begin by looking at articles by Stewart, noting their structure and the kinds of suggestions they offer, and then brainstorm exaggerated Stewart-like suggestions. Here's an example of one such parody:

> Martha Stewart Holiday Calendar
>
> December 6 Fax family Christmas newsletter to Pulitzer committee for consideration.
>
> December 9 Record own Christmas album complete with 4 part harmony and all instrument accompaniment performed by myself. Mail to all my friends and loved ones.
>
> December 21 Drain city reservoir; refill with mulled cider, orange slices and cinnamon sticks.
>
> December 25 Bear son. Swaddle. Lay in color coordinated manger scented with homemade potpourri.
>
> December 27 Build snowman in exact likeness of God. (Sultanoff)

Although this parody pokes fun at the particular domestic pretense of Stewart, it's generally on target for all of the articles that seem bent on either creating that perfect holiday or making us all feel inadequate about our imperfect ones. Students might consider a similar calendar but from other exaggerated points of view.

➢ Create a parody list of summer vacation suggestions from an obsessive sports coach, controlling parent, or exacting English teacher.

Advice columns that combine a topic with a seemingly incompatible context can often be quite funny. For example, we might consider the chapter "Dress to Intimidate: Personal Grooming and Fashion Tips for the Post-Apocalypse" found in *Field Guide to the Apocalypse* by Meghann Marco. It begins,

> How you present yourself to what's left of humanity is of the utmost importance. Now, more than ever, first impressions matter. Your wardrobe must be durable, practical, and terrifying. You must always look as if you have just ambushed someone on the side of the road, snapped his neck with your bare hands, stolen his car, and fed his liver to your dog. Your dog must look as if he'd like another liver. (55)

- Brainstorm a list of situations and ill-corresponding types of advice: for example, being stranded on a desert island and home decor advice, or living on a space station and bird-hunting tips. Create a short advice article for this type of scenario.

Of more direct appeal to secondary students might be the how-to-attract-the-perfect guy/gal article. Many students will be quite familiar with this subgenre because they encounter examples in nearly every magazine from *Cosmo Girl* to *Esquire*. Along the same lines, teen magazine quizzes—"Are You a Flirt? Take Our Quiz and Find Out!"—offer wonderful opportunities to pan a well-deserving format. In fact, a class project to collectively create a parody of a teen magazine, from cover to advertisements to articles, would offer an opportunity to explore everything from graphic design to persuasion and marketing techniques to the construction of a feature article.

- Create a parody article for one of the following topics: a makeover, advice on muscle toning, a fashion upgrade, flirty moves, opening lines, or some other topic typical of magazines aimed at young adults.
- Create a parody of a teen magazine quiz.
- Create a parody of a teen magazine cover.

"Authentic" Adolescent Nonfiction

Finally, students might create parodies of the kinds of nonfiction texts that some of them are already writing.

- Choose one of the following, and create a parody version with either a perfect or rather imperfect candidate.
    - Class president campaign speech
    - College application essay (see http://urbanlegends.about.com/library/blbyol3.htm for the most famous example)
    - Summer job résumé

Each of these parodies offers a back door into a discussion of what should go into such texts and how they should be structured.

And don't forget that the social-networking texts that so many students are obsessed with deserve some parodic attention.

- As a class, construct a fake MySpace or Facebook page for a stereotypical teenager.
- Create an exaggerated version of a *twittered* day-in-the-life of a high school student in one-hundred-words-or-less bursts.

Finally, of course, invite your students to come up with their own ideas for parodying the texts that they see around them.

Note

1. *The Onion* articles can be found in these issues: "Spain Vows Eternal Vigilance in War on Bulls," 3 Nov. 2004; "Elderly Man Skipping Work Uses 'Dead Grandson' Excuse Again," 10 June 2009; "KFC No Longer Permitted to Use Word 'Eat' in Advertisements,'" 26 May 2009; "Elf Finger Found in Box of Keebler Cookies," 14 Sept. 2005; and "Kobe Bryant Proves He Can Win Championship with Luke Walton on Team," 18 June 2009.

Works Cited and Useful Teacher Resources

All of these sources have useful ideas and examples, but many of them also have material that is likely not suitable for some classrooms. Discretion and previewing are advised.

Abish, Walter. *Alphabetical Africa*. New York: New Directions, 1974. Print.

Aciman, Alexander, and Emmett Rensin. *Twitterature: The World's Greatest Books in Twenty Tweets or Less*. New York: Penguin, 2009. Print.

Adcock, Siobhan, ed. "Aspiring DJ" *Hipster Haiku*. New York: Broadway, 2006. 11. Print.

Addictionary. Web. 15 Dec. 2010.

Alexie, Sherman. *The Absolutely True Diary of a Part-Time Indian*. New York: Little, 2007. Print.

———. *The Business of Fancydancing*. New York: Hanging Loose, 1992. Print.

Allen, Woody. "Selections from the Allen Notebooks." *Fierce Pajamas: An Anthology of Humor Writing from the New Yorker*. Eds. David Remnick and Henry Finder. New York: Modern Library, 2002. 231–34. Print.

Anderson, Laurie Halse. *Speak*. New York: Puffin, 1999. Print.

Armour, Richard. *Punctured Poems: Famous First and Infamous Second Lines*. Santa Barbara, CA: Woodbridge, 1982. Print.

———. *Writing Light Verse and Prose Humor*. Boston: Writer, 1971. Print.

Austen, Jane and Seth Grahame-Smith. *Pride and Prejudice and Zombies*. Philadelphia: Quirk, 2009. Print.

Baker, Kenneth, ed. *Unauthorized Versions: Poems and Their Parodies*. New York: Faber, 1990. Print.

Baker, Russell, ed. *The Norton Book of Light Verse*. New York: Norton, 1986. Print.

Barry, Dave. *Dave Barry Is Not Taking This Sitting Down*. New York: Ballentine, 2000. Print.

———. *Dave Barry Slept Here: A Sort of History of the United States*. New York: Ballentine, 1997. Print.

———. *Dave Barry's Complete Guide to Guys*. New York: Ballentine, 1995. Print.

Beard, Henry. "Hamlet's Cat's Soliloquy." *Poetry for Cats: The Definitive Anthology of Distinguished Feline Verse*. New York: Villard, 1994. 8–9. Print.

Beatty, Paul, ed. *Hokum: An Anthology of African-American Humor*. New York: Bloomsbury, 2006. Print.

Berk, Ronald A. *Humor as an Instructional Defibrillator: Evidence-Based Techniques in Teaching and Assessment*. Sterling, VA: Stylus, 2002. Print.

———. *Professors Are from Mars, Students Are from Snickers: How to Write and Deliver Humor in the Classroom and in Professional Presentations*. Sterling, VA: Stylus, 2003. Print.

Bernard, Ian. *Writing Humor: Giving a Comedic Touch to All Forms of Writing*. Santa Barbara, CA: Capra, 2003. Print.

Bevington, Helen. "The Princess and the Pea." *American Wits: An Anthology of Light Verse*. New York: Library of American, 2003. 40. Print.

Bierce, Ambrose. *The Devil's Dictionary*. [1906]. *Project Gutenberg*. Web. 15 Dec. 2010.

Brandreth, Gyles. *The Joy of Lex: How to Have Fun with 860,341,500 Words*. New York: Quill, 1983. Print.

Breen, Jon. *Hair of the Sleuthhound: Parodies of Mystery Fiction*. Metuchen, NJ: Scarecrow, 1982. Print.

Brooks, Max. *The Zombie Survival Guide: Complete Protection from the Living Dead*. New York: Three Rivers, 2003. Print.

Brooks, Mel, dir. *Blazing Saddles*. Warner Brothers, 1974. Film.

Brownlee, Liz. *Liz Brownlee Poet*. Web. 15 Dec. 2010.

———. "Shoem." *Read Me and Laugh: A Funny Poem for Every Day of the Year*. Ed. Gaby Morgan. London: MacMillan, 2005. 300–301. Print.

Carroll, Lewis. *Through the Looking-Glass*. *Project Gutenberg*. Web. Mar. 18 2011.

Carroll, Lewis. "Jabberwocky." *Bartleby.com*. Web. 18 Mar. 2011.

Carter, Judy. *The Comedy Bible: From Stand-Up to Sitcom—The Comedy Writer's Ultimate How-to Guide*. New York: Fireside, 2001. Print.

Cary, Stephen. *Working with English Language Learners: Answers to Teachers' Top Ten Questions*. 2nd Ed. Portsmouth, NH: Heinemann, 2007. Print.

Chace, H. L. "Ladle Rat Rotten Hut." *Exploratorium*. Web. 18 Mar. 2011.

Chandler, Raymond. *The Big Sleep; Farewell, My Lovely; The High Window*. New York: Everyman's, 2002. 199–442. Print.

———. *Raymond Chandler: Later Novels and Other Writings: The Lady in the Lake / The Little Sister / The Long Goodbye / Playback / Double Indemnity / Selected Essays and Letters*. Ed. Frank McShane. New York: Library of America, 2002. 201–416. Print.

Chast, Roz. "Romeo and Juliet Text Messages." *Web English Teacher*. Web. 18 Mar. 2011.

"Cliché Finder." *Westegg.com*. Web. 15 Dec. 2010.

Clifton, Lucille. "Homage to My Hips." *Good Woman: Poems and a Memoir 1969–1980*. Rochester, NY: BOA, 1987. 168. Print.

Cole, William, ed. *Poem Stew*. New York: Harper, 1981. Print.

Collins, Billy. "Litany." *Nine Horses: Poems*. New York: Random, 2003. 69–70. Print.

Conley, Darby. "Get Fuzzy." Comic Strip. *Seattle Times* 1 July 2009. Print.

Cope, Wendy, ed. *The Funny Side: 101 Humorous Poems*. London: Faber, 1998. Print.

———. *Serious Concerns*. London: Faber, 1992. Print.

Cornett, Claudia. *Learning through Laughter . . . Again*. Bloomington, IN: Phi Delta Kappa, 2001. Print.

Dalzell, Tom. *Flappers 2 Rappers: American Youth Slang*. Springfield, MA: Merriam-Webster, 1996. Print.

Davis, Murray S. *What's So Funny? The Comic Conception of Culture and Society*. Chicago: U of Chicago P, 1993. Print.

Denny, Alma. "Mrs Hobson's Choice." *The Funny Side: 100 Humorous Poems*. Ed. Wendy Cope. London: Faber, 1998. 28. Print.

"Doctor's Advice." *Medijokes.com*. Web. 18 Mar. 2011.

"Dog Haiku." *More Happy Pet Poems*. Wed. 14 Apr. 2011. <http://www.unicorn-chinese-cresteds.com/poems2.html>.

Dougherty, Barry, and H. Aaron Cohl, eds. *The Friars Club Encyclopedia of Jokes*. New York: Black Dog and Leventhal, 2009. Print.

Dumas, Firoozeh. *Funny in Farsi: A Memoir of Growing Up Iranian in America*. New York: Random, 2003. Print.

Dyckman, Jay. "RE: Hardy Boys Manuscript Submission." *The McSweeney's Joke Book of Book Jokes*. New York: Vintage, 2008. 23–24. Print.

Eliot, T. S. *Old Possum's Book of Practical Cats*. New York: Harcourt, 1939. Print.

Ewart, Gavin. *The Gavin Ewart Show: Selected Poems 1939–1985*. Cleveland, OH: Bits, 1986. Print.

"Eye Halve a Spelling Chequer." *Learn English–British Council*. Web. 18 Mar. 2011.

Fishback, Margaret. *One to a Customer: Collected Poems*. New York: Dutton, 1940. Print.

Fisher, David. *Legally Correct Fairy Tales*. New York: Warner, 1996. Print.

Fried, Katrina, and Lena Tabori, eds. *The Little Big Book of Laughter*. New York: Welcome, 2004. Print.

Gardner, Martin, ed. *Martin Gardner's Favorite Poetic Parodies*. Amherst, NY: Prometheus, 2002. Print.

Garner, James Finn. *Politically Correct Bedtime Stories*. New York: MacMillan, 1994. Print.

Gerber, Michael. *Barry Trotter and the Unauthorized Parody*. New York: Fireside, 2002. Print.

Getlen, Larry, ed. *The Complete Idiot's Guide to Jokes*. New York: Alpha, 2006. Print.

Ginsberg, Allen. *Howl and Other Poems*. San Francisco, CA: City Lights, 1956. Print.

Green, John. *Looking for Alaska*. New York: Speak, 2005. Print.

"Green Eggs and Hamlet." *Rec.Humor.Funny Jokes*. Web. 18 Mar. 2011. <http://www.netfunny.com/rhf/jokes/97/May/geandh.html>.

Greenwell, Bill. "Dover Beach." *Bill Greenwell's Site*. Web. 15 Dec. 2010. <http://www.billgreenwell.com/poems/display_poem.php?key_id=509>.

"Haiku DOS." Web. 14 Apr. 2011. <http://www.esp.org/humor/poetry.pdf.>

Hall, Donald, ed. *The Oxford Book of Children's Verse in America*. New York: Oxford UP, 1985. Print.

Handey, Jack. "The Voices in My Head." *Flash Fiction Forward: 80 Very Short Stories*. Ed. James Thomas and Robert Shapard. New York: Norton, 2006. 85–87. Print.

Harry's Bar and American Grill. *Best of Bad Hemingway: Vol. 1: Choice Entries from the Harry's Bar and Grill Imitation Hemingway Competition*. San Diego, CA: Harcourt, 1989. Print.

Helitzer, Melvin. *Comedy Writing Secrets: How to Think Funny, Write Funny, Act Funny and Get Paid for It*. Cincinnati, OH: Writer's Digest, 1987. Print.

Hemingway, Ernest. *The Sun Also Rises*. 1926. New York: Scribner, 2006. Print.

Hollander, John, ed. *American Wits: An Anthology of Light Verse*. New York: Library of American, 2003. Print.

Jacobs, A. J. *Fractured Fairy Tales*. New York: Bantam, 1999. Print.

"Jargon Watch." *Wired Magazine*. April 1996. Web. 18 Mar. 2011.

Jerome, Jerome K. *Three Men in a Boat (To Say Nothing of the Dog)*. London, 1889. *Project Gutenberg*. Web. Apr. 22, 2010.

Kachuba, John B., ed. *How to Write Funny*. Cincinnati, OH: Writer's Digest, 2001. Print.

Keeler, Greg. "Duct Tape Psalm." *American Falls*. Lewiston, ID: Confluence, 1987. 61. Print.

———. "Swiss Army Sermon." *Epiphany at Goofy's Gas*. Livingston, MT: Clark City, 1991. 106. Print.

Keillor, Garrison. "Guy Noir." *A Prairie Home Companion*. 30 Nov. 2002. Web. 18 Mar. 2011.

"KFC No Longer Permitted to Use Word 'Eat' in Advertisements." *The Onion*. 26 May 2009. Web. 8 Apr. 2011.

Kher, Neelam, Susan Molstad, and Roberta Donahue. "Using Humor in the College Classroom to Enhance Teaching Effectiveness in 'Dread Courses.'" *College Student Journal* 33.3 (1999): 400–407.

Koertge, Ron. *Stoner and Spaz*. Cambridge, MA: Candlewick, 2002. Print.

Lanham, Robert. "Internet-Age Writing Syllabus and Course Overview." *McSweeney's*. Web. 15 Dec. 2010.

Lansky, Bruce. "How to Write a Newfangled Tongue Twister." *Giggle Poetry*. Web. 15 Dec. 2010.

Lederer, Richard. *Anguished English: An Anthology of Accidental Assaults Upon Our Language*. New York: Laurel, 1987. Print.

Letterman, David. "Top Ten Signs You're Watching a Bad Monster Movie." 18 Jan. 2008. *CBS.com*. Late Show with David Letterman Top Ten Archive. Web. 15 Dec. 2010.

LOL Cat Bible Translation Project. Web. 18 Mar. 2011.

Mac, Bernie. "Pass the Milk." *African American Humor: The Best Black Comedy from Slavery to Today*. Ed. Mel Watkins. Chicago: Lawrence Hill, 2002. 312. Print.

"Malapropism." *Wikipedia*. Web. 28 Mar. 2011.

Marco, Meghann. *Field Guide to the Apocalypse: Movie Survival Skills for the End of the World*. New York: Simon, 2005. Print.

Martin, Rod A. *The Psychology of Humor: An Integrative Approach*. Boston: Elsevier Academic, 2007. Print.

Martin, Steve. "Steve Martin Onstage." *New York Magazine* 22 Aug. 1977: 49. Print.

McGinley, Phyllis. *Times Three: Selected Verse from Three Decades*. New York: Viking, 1961. Print.

McGough, Roger, ed. *The Kingfisher Book of Funny Poems*. New York: Kingfisher, 2002. Print.

McManus, Patrick F. "My First Deer, and Welcome to It." *They Shoot Canoes, Don't They?* New York: Holt, 1981. 54–61. Print.

———. "Skunk Dog." *They Shoot Canoes, Don't They?* New York: Holt, 1981. 18–25. Print

Mecum, Ryan. *Zombie Haiku*. Cincinnati, OH: How, 2008. Print.

Mendrinos, James. *The Complete Idiot's Guide to Comedy Writing*. New York: Alpha, 2004. Print.

Merriam, Eve. *It Doesn't Always Have to Rhyme*. New York: Atheneum, 1964. Print.

Montgomery, Lucy Maud. *Anne of Green Gables*. [1908]. *Project Gutenberg*. Web. 22 Apr. 2010.

Morgan, Gaby, ed. *Read Me and Laugh: A Funny Poem for Every Day of the Year*. London: MacMillan, 2005. Print.

Morrison, Mary Kay. *Using Humor to Maximize Learning: The Links Between Positive Emotions and Education*. Lanham, MD: Rowman, 2008. Print.

Nash, Ogden. "Everybody Tells Me Everything." *The Best of Ogden Nash*. Ed. Linell Nash Smith. Chicago: Dee, 2007. 383. Print.

Nason, Cheryl. *The Fun Factor: Your Prescription for Stress Relief at Work and at Home*. New York: Core, 2005. Print.

Norvig, Peter. "The Gettysburg Powerpoint Presentation." *Norvig.com*. Web. 15 Dec. 2010.

Novak, William, and Moshe Waldoks, eds. *The Big Book of New American Humor*. New York: Harper, 1990. Print.

The Onion. Web. 15 Dec. 2010.

Padgett, Ron, ed. *The Teachers and Writers Handbook of Poetic Forms*. New York: Teachers and Writers, 1987. Print.

Paris, Roxanne. "An Open (Love) Letter to Taco Bell's Crunchwrap Supreme." *McSweeney's*. 3 May 2006. Web. 15 Dec. 2010.

Parker, Dorothy. *Complete Poems*. New York: Penguin, 2010. Print.

Parrot, E. O., ed. *How to Be Well-Versed in Poetry*. New York: Penguin, 1990. Print.

Peck, Dennis. "Friday's Edge: Taking the Class out of the Classics, Part Deux." *Oregonian*. 7 Aug. 2009: E3. Print.

Perret, Gene. *Comedy Writing Workbook*. Studio City, CA: Players, 1994. Print.

———. *The New Comedy Writing: Step by Step*. Sanger, CA: Quill Driver, 2007. Print.

Pollock, Michael. *How to Write Funny Lyrics: The Comedy Songwriting Manual*. Hollywood, CA: Masteryear, 2006. Print.

Post, Jonathan Vos. "Raymond Chandler's Hamlet." Web. 18 Mar. 2011.

Powell, Joseph, and Mark Halperin. *Accent on Meter: A Handbook for Readers of Poetry*. Urbana, IL: NCTE, 2004. Print.

Radner, Gilda. "The Deaf Penalty." *The Big Book of New American Humor*. Ed. William Novak and Moshe Waldoks. New York: Harper, 1990. 63. Print.

"Ray Charles." *Urban Dictionary*. Web. 15 Dec. 2010.

Regan, Patrick, ed. *Teachers: Jokes, Quotes, and Anecdotes*. New York: Barnes and Noble, 2004. Print.

Reid, Luc. *Talk the Talk: The Slang of 65 American Subcultures*. New York: Fall River, 2009. Print.

Richardson-Bryan, Mike. "Klingon Fairy Tales." *The McSweeney's Joke Book of Book Jokes*. New York: Vintage, 2008. 53–54. Print.

Rock, Chris. *Rock This!* New York: Hyperion, 2000. Print.

Rogauskas, James. *Office Haiku: Poems Inspired by the Daily Grind*. New York: St. Martin's, 2006. Print.

Rowling, J. K. *Harry Potter and the Sorcerer's Stone*. New York: Scholastic, 1999. Print.

Salinger, J. D. *The Catcher in the Rye*. New York: Little, 1951. Print.

Schreiber, Brad. *What Are You Laughing At? How to Write Funny Screenplays, Stories and More*. Studio City, CA: Wiese, 2003. Print.

Scieszka, Jon. *The True Story of the Three Little Pigs*. New York: Puffin, 1996.

———. *The Stinky Cheese Man and Other Fairly Stupid Tales*. New York: Viking, 1992. Print.

Sedita, Scott. *The Eight Characters of Comedy: A Guide to Sitcom Acting and Writing*. Los Angeles: Atides, 2006. Print.

Service, Robert William. "The Cremation of Sam McGee." *PoemHunter.com*. Web. 19 May 2010.

Shade, Richard. "Humor: A Course of Study for Gifted Learners." *Gifted Child Today* 22(1), 46–49. Print.

Shakespeare, William. *Hamlet*. Act Three, Scene One. *Project Gutenberg*. Web. 18 Mar. 2011.

Shapiro, Karen Jo. *Because I Could Not Stop My Bike and Other Poems*. Watertown, MA: Charlesbridge, 2005. Print.

———. *I Must Go Down to the Beach Again and Other Poems*. Watertown, MA: Charlesbridge, 2007. Print.

Silverstein, Shel. *Where the Sidewalk Ends: The Poems and Drawings of Shel Silverstein*. New York: Harper, 1974. Print.

"Similes and Metaphors." *Grammarbook.com*.Web. 14 Apr. 2011. <http://data.grammarbook.com/blog/effective-writing/similes-and-metaphors>.

Smith, Michael W., and Jeffrey D. Wilhelm. *"Reading Don't Fix No Chevys": Literacy in the Lives of Young Men*. Portsmouth, NH: Heinemann, 2002. Print.

Suddath, Claire. "An Open Letter to the Totally Impractical Size Chart for Women's Clothing." *McSweeney's*. 26 May 2005. Web. 15 Dec. 2010.

Sultanoff, Steven M. "Martha Stewart Holiday Calendar." *Humor Matters*. Web. 15 Dec. 2010.

Thurber, James. "The Secret Life of Walter Mitty." *The Thurber Carnival*. New York: Harper, 1999. 55–60. Print.

———. "A Visit from Saint Nicholas (In the Ernest Hemingway Manner)." *New Yorker*. 24 Dec. 1927. 17. Print.

Tibbals, Geoff, ed. *The Mammoth Book of Jokes*. Philadelphia: Running, 2006. Print.

Trillin, Calvin. *A Heckuva Job: More of the Bush Administration in Rhyme*. New York: Random, 2006. Print.

Twain, Mark. *Adventures of Huckleberry Finn. Electronic Text Center, University of Virginia Library*. Web. 18 Mar. 2011.

———. "The Story of the Bad Little Boy." *Mark Twain's Sketches, New and Old*. Hartford, CT: American, 1882. *Project Gutenberg*. 5 Dec. 2010. Web. 8 Apr. 2011.

"Twists, Slug and Roscoes: A glossary of Hardboiled Slang." *Miskatonic University Press*. Web. 18 Mar. 2011.

Vorhaus, John. *The Comic Toolbox: How to Be Funny Even If You're Not*. Los Angeles: Silman, 1994. Print.

Watterson, Bill. *The Complete Calvin and Hobbes: Book Two*. Kansas City: Andrews McMeel, 2005. 153. Print.

Welch, Pat. *Catku: What is the Sound of One Cat Napping*. Kansas City, MO: Andrews, 2004. Print.

Wells, Dean Faulkner, ed. *The Best of Bad Faulkner: Choice Entries from the Faux Faulkner Competition*. San Diego, CA: Harcourt, 1991. Print.

Williams, William Carlos. "This is Just to Say." *William Carlos Williams: Selected Poems*. Ed. Charles Tomlinson. New York: New Directions, 1985. 74. Print.

Wright, Sylvia. "The Death of Lady Mondegreen." *Harper's Magazine* Nov. 1954: 48–51. Print.

"Young America's News Source: Jon Stewart." *CNN.com*. 2 Mar. 2004. Web. 18 Mar. 2011.

Zaranka, William, ed. *The Brand-X Anthology of Poetry: A Parody Anthology*. Cambridge, MA: Apple-Wood, 1981. Print.

———, ed. *Brand X Fiction: A Parody Anthology*. London: Picador, 1984. Print.

Ziv, Avner. "Teaching and Learning with Humor: Experiment and Replication." *Journal of Experimental Education* 57.1 (1988): 5–15. Print.

Index

Author

Bruce A. Goebel, previously a secondary English teacher, now teaches in the Department of English at Western Washington University, where he offers courses on humor, American literature, young adult literature, and English teaching methods. He is the author of *Reading Native American Literature: A Teacher's Guide* (2004) and coeditor (with James C. Hall) of *Teaching a "New Canon"? Students, Teachers, and Texts in the College Literature Classroom* (1995). In 2010, he received an honorable mention for the Edwin M. Hopkins Award for his article "Comic Relief: Engaging Students through Humor Writing."